Designing for Digital Reading

Synthesis Lectures on Information Concepts, Retrieval, and Services

Editor
Gary Marchionini, *University of North Carolina, Chapel Hill*

Designing for Digital Reading
Jennifer Pearson, George Buchanan, and Harold Thimbleby
2013

Information Retrieval Models: Foundations and Relationships
Thomas Roelleke
2013

Key Issues Regarding Digital Libraries: Evaluation and Integration
Rao Shen, Marcos André Gonçalves, and Edward A. Fox
2013

Visual Information Retrieval using Java and LIRE
Mathias Lux and Oge Marques
2013

On the Efficient Determination of Most Near Neighbors: Horseshoes, Hand Grenades,
Web Search and Other Situations When Close is Close Enough
Mark S. Manasse
2012

The Answer Machine
Susan E. Feldman
2012

Theoretical Foundations for Digital Libraries: The 5S (Societies, Scenarios, Spaces,
Structures, Streams) Approach
Edward A. Fox, Marcos André Gonçalves, and Rao Shen
2012

The Future of Personal Information Management, Part I: Our Information, Always and Forever
William Jones
2012

Search User Interface Design
Max L. Wilson
2011

Information Retrieval Evaluation
Donna Harman
2011

Knowledge Management (KM) Processes in Organizations: Theoretical Foundations and Practice
Claire R. McInerney and Michael E. D. Koenig
2011

Search-Based Applications: At the Confluence of Search and Database Technologies
Gregory Grefenstette and Laura Wilber
2010

Information Concepts: From Books to Cyberspace Identities
Gary Marchionini
2010

Estimating the Query Difficulty for Information Retrieval
David Carmel and Elad Yom-Tov
2010

iRODS Primer: Integrated Rule-Oriented Data System
Arcot Rajasekar, Reagan Moore, Chien-Yi Hou, Christopher A. Lee, Richard Marciano, Antoine de Torcy, Michael Wan, Wayne Schroeder, Sheau-Yen Chen, Lucas Gilbert, Paul Tooby, and Bing Zhu
2010

Collaborative Web Search: Who, What, Where, When, and Why
Meredith Ringel Morris and Jaime Teevan
2009

Multimedia Information Retrieval
Stefan Rüger
2009

Online Multiplayer Games
William Sims Bainbridge
2009

Information Architecture: The Design and Integration of Information Spaces
Wei Ding and Xia Lin
2009

Reading and Writing the Electronic Book
Catherine C. Marshall
2009

Hypermedia Genes: An Evolutionary Perspective on Concepts, Models, and Architectures
Nuno M. Guimarães and Luís M. Carrico
2009

Understanding User-Web Interactions via Web Analytics
Bernard J. (Jim) Jansen
2009

XML Retrieval
Mounia Lalmas
2009

Faceted Search
Daniel Tunkelang
2009

Introduction to Webometrics: Quantitative Web Research for the Social Sciences
Michael Thelwall
2009

Exploratory Search: Beyond the Query-Response Paradigm
Ryen W. White and Resa A. Roth
2009

New Concepts in Digital Reference
R. David Lankes
2009

Automated Metadata in Multimedia Information Systems: Creation, Refinement, Use in Surrogates, and Evaluation
Michael G. Christel
2009

Designing for Digital Reading

Jennifer Pearson, George Buchanan, and Harold Thimbleby

ISBN: 978-3-031-01202-0   paperback
ISBN: 978-3-031-02330-9   ebook

DOI 10.1007/978-3-031-02330-9

A Publication in the Springer series
SYNTHESIS LECTURES ON INFORMATION CONCEPTS, RETRIEVAL, AND SERVICES

Lecture #29
Series Editor: Gary Marchionini, *University of North Carolina, Chapel Hill*
Series ISSN
Synthesis Lectures on Information Concepts, Retrieval, and Services
Print 1947-945X   Electronic 1947-9468

Designing for Digital Reading

Jennifer Pearson
Swansea University, Wales, UK

George Buchanan
City University, London, UK

Harold Thimbleby
Swansea University, Wales, UK

SYNTHESIS LECTURES ON INFORMATION CONCEPTS, RETRIEVAL, AND SERVICES #29

ABSTRACT

Reading is a complex human activity that has evolved, and co-evolved, with technology over thousands of years. Mass printing in the fifteenth century firmly established what we know as the modern book, with its physical format of covers and paper pages, and now-standard features such as page numbers, footnotes, and diagrams. Today, electronic documents are enabling paperless reading supported by eReading technologies such as Kindles and Nooks, yet a high proportion of users still opt to print on paper before reading. This persistent habit of 'printing to read' is one sign of the shortcomings of digital documents—although the popularity of eReaders is one sign of the shortcomings of paper. How do we get the best of both worlds?

The physical properties of paper (for example, it is light, thin, and flexible) contribute to the ease with which physical documents are manipulated; but these properties have a completely different set of affordances to their digital equivalents. Paper can be folded, ripped, or scribbled on almost subconsciously—activities that require significant cognitive attention in their digital form, if they are even possible. The nearly subliminal interaction that comes from years of learned behavior with paper has been described as *lightweight interaction*, which is achieved when a person actively reads an article in a way that is so easy and unselfconscious that they are not apt to remember their actions later.

Reading is now in a period of rapid change, and digital text is fast becoming the predominant mode of reading. As a society, we are merely at the start of the journey of designing truly effective tools for handling digital text.

This book investigates the advantages of paper, how the affordances of paper can be realized in digital form, and what forms best support lightweight interaction for active reading. To understand how to design for the future, we review the ways reading technology and reader behavior have both changed and remained constant over hundreds of years. We explore the reasoning behind reader behavior and introduce and evaluate several user interface designs that implement these lightweight properties familiar from our everyday use of paper.

We start by looking back, reviewing the development of reading technology and the progress of research on reading over many years. Drawing key concepts from this review, we move forward to develop and test methods for creating new and more effective interactions for supporting digital reading. Finally, we lay down a set of lightweight attributes which can be used as evidence-based guidelines to improve the usability of future digital reading technologies. By the end of this book, then, we hope you will be equipped to critique the present state of digital reading, and to better design and evaluate new interaction styles and technologies.

KEYWORDS

reading, active reading, documents, eReaders, annotation, bookmarking, note-taking, indexing, books, digital libraries

i Mamgu
for Granny

Contents

Preface xv

Acknowledgments xvii

Figure Credits xix

1 Introduction 1
    1.1   Outline of This Book 4
    1.2   Who Should Read This Book? 6

2 Reading Through the Ages 7
    2.1   A Brief History of Reading 7
        2.1.1   Scribes and Scholars 7
        2.1.2   Mechanical Printing 11
        2.1.3   Electronic Printing 12
        2.1.4   Evolution for the Reader 13
        2.1.5   Images and Figures 15
    2.2   From Print to Digital Reading 16
        2.2.1   The Era of Digital Publication 17
        2.2.2   Hypertext and Online Reading 17
        2.2.3   eReaders and eBooks 18
        2.2.4   Digital Rights Management 20
    2.3   The State of the Art 21
        2.3.1   The Visual Book Metaphor 22
        2.3.2   Page Display 23
        2.3.3   Realistic Book Software 24
        2.3.4   The Affordances of Paper Project 27
        2.3.5   Augmented Reading Hardware 28
    2.4   Future Developments 29
    2.5   Summary 31

3   Key Concepts **33**

　3.1   Reading 33

　　3.1.1   Active Reading 33

　　3.1.2   Reading in Conjunction with Writing 34

　　3.1.3   On-screen Reading 35

　　3.1.4   Reading and Cognition 36

　3.2   Lightweight Interaction 38

　　3.2.1   Paper versus Digital 39

　3.3   Cognition and the User 39

　　3.3.1   Ready-to-Hand and Present-at-Hand 39

　　3.3.2   Invisible Computers 40

　　3.3.3   Flow 40

　　3.3.4   Distraction 41

　　3.3.5   Affordance 42

　　3.3.6   Metaphors 43

　3.4   Summary 44

4   Lightweight Interactions **47**

　4.1   Introduction 47

　4.2   Placeholders 47

　　4.2.1   Background 48

　　4.2.2   Lightweight Placeholders 53

　　4.2.3   Lightweight Properties 54

　4.3   Annotations 57

　　4.3.1   Background 58

　　4.3.2   Lightweight Annotations 65

　　4.3.3   Lightweight Properties 67

　4.4   Note-taking 69

　　4.4.1   Background 69

　　4.4.2   Lightweight Note-taking 73

　　4.4.3   Lightweight Properties 77

　4.5   Visual Indexing 79

　　4.5.1   Background 79

　　4.5.2   Current Methods 80

　　4.5.3   Lightweight Indexing 84

　　4.5.4   Lightweight Properties 89

5   Improving Digital Reading **93**

    5.1   Overview 93

    5.2   Running Themes 95

        5.2.1 Additional Space 95

        5.2.2 Visual Language 96

        5.2.3 Immediacy of Access 97

        5.2.4 Digital Technologies 98

        5.2.5 Designing for Appropriation 98

        5.2.6 Completeness of Metaphors 98

    5.3   The Book Metaphor 99

    5.4   Electronic Documents 100

    5.5   Concluding Remarks 102

Bibliography **105**

Authors' Biographies **115**

Preface

Together, we have spent six years exploring how to make digital reading a better experience. We have each found frustration at using the current "state-of-the-art" technologies, and at the same time understood how this poor design was not necessary. Reading can be for fun, learning, or relaxation, but we all believe that the experience should be more about the text and the journey it takes the reader on, than fighting with poor quality print, a springing spine, or, more often, a difficult user interface.

Today, as electronic books are becoming evermore ingrained and implanted into our daily lives, we all find ourselves reading more frequently on screen. Whether it be to undertake active reading on a PC workstation or enjoy a novel on an eReader, the act of reading is shifting more and more toward the digital, making it an opportune time to investigate the on-screen reading process.

While investigating how to improve reading, we have implemented several lightweight active reading tools, and consequently evaluated them. We don't claim that our solutions are the best, last word. Indeed, we rather hope not. Many other researchers are also making substantial contributions to a valuable cause of improving what is, for many, an everyday activity. We have very much enjoyed our work, and been stimulated by others. Hopefully this book will also excite and inform you, and, perhaps, you too will be able to add your own ideas in the future to help us all make reading on digital devices the delight many have found reading to be in print.

Jennifer Pearson, George Buchanan, and Harold Thimbleby
October 2013

Acknowledgments

We would like to thank many friends and colleagues who have helped us in preparing this book. The team at the Future Interaction Laboratory at Swansea University, particularly Matt Jones, Simon Robinson, Tom Owen, and Patrick Oladimeji, helped immensely with drafting not only this book, but in preparing papers and research along the way. Victoria Hurst has helped frequently and effectively with all sorts of unexpected issues and practicalities. We would also like to thank our reviewers and Gary Marchionini for their helpful comments to improve and refine the content of this volume. There are also many people who have offered friendly encouragement and support over the course of this process. Thanks too, then, to Laura, Ann, Phil, Hannah, Thomas, Susie, David, Ben, Emma, and Wende.

Finally we would like to express our gratitude to Microsoft Research Cambridge, particularly Richard Harper, and the Department of Computer Science at Swansea University, for the financial support they have offered throughout the research that led to this book.

Thanks, everyone!

Jen George Harol

Figure Credits

Figure 3.1   Based on Csikszentmihalyi M. (1998). *Finding flow: The psychology of engagement with everyday life.* New York, NY: Basic Books. Copyright © 1997, Perseus Books Group. ISBN: 9780465024117.

Figure 4.5   From Buchanan and Pearson. Improving Placeholders in Digital Documents. In Proceedings from the 12th European Conference on Research and Advanced Technology for Digital Libraries, volume 5173 of ECDL '08, pages 1–12. Springer Berlin/Heidelberg, 2008. DOI: 10.1007/978-3-540-87599-4_1.

Figure 4.6   From *CliffsComplete Macbeth.* Copyright © 2000, Houghton Mifflin Harcourt Publishing Company. Used with permission. ISBN: 9780764585722

Figures 4.10   From Pearson, et al. Improving Annotations in Digital Documents. In Proceedings of the 13th European Conference on Research and Advanced Technology for Digital Libraries, volume 5714 of ECDL '09, pages 429–432. Springer Berlin/Heidelberg, 2009. DOI: 10.1007/978-3-642-04346-8_51

Figures 4.11 and 4.13   From Pearson, et al. The Digital Reading Desk: A Lightweight Approach to Digital Note-Taking. Interacting with Computers, 24(5):327–338, 2012b. DOI: 10.1016/j.intcom.2012.03.001.

Figures 4.18   From Pearson, et al. Creating Visualisations for Digital Document Indexing. In Proceedings from the 13th European Conference on Research and Advanced Technology for Digital Libraries, volume 5714 of ECDL '09, pages 87–93. Springer Berlin/Heidelberg, 2009b. DOI: 10.1007/978-3-642-04346-8_10.

CHAPTER 1

Introduction

The advent of the personal computer brought predictions of the so-called 'paperless office' [Sellen and Harper, 2003], promising the elimination of paper from everyday office-related tasks. Twenty years on from this original prediction [BusinessWeek, June 30, 1975] digital documents are becoming more and more portable with the introduction of eReaders and mobile multi-function devices such as iPads [Wahba, September 22, 2010]. New release novels and articles which were once bound to paper are now available for download in an instant, direct from online retailers, revolutionizing digital reading. Even in the relatively short time we have been working on this book, the uptake of documents in digital form has significantly increased. In fact, the use of digital documents has increased so much that in July 2010 Amazon announced that for the first time it had sold more Kindle books than both paper and hard backs for the top 10, 100, and 1,000 best-selling books on its U.S. website amazon.com [BBC News, January 28, 2011; The New York Times, July 19, 2010]. It was also announced, in 2011, that the prestigious Man Booker Prize would be digitized for the first time by giving the judges eReaders instead of piles of physical books [BBC News, January 28, 2011].

This substantial increase in digital document uptake means it is timely to investigate the issues surrounding reading in its electronic form. There are many examples where on-screen reading tools have proven themselves deficient compared to their physical equivalents [Marshall and Bly, 2005; O'Hara and Sellen, 1997], an issue that, if left unresolved, could hinder the continued growth of digital document use. This book explores current tools designed to aid the on-screen reading process and improves upon them by incorporating lightweight techniques that pose a minimal intrusion on the primary reading task. By doing so, we aim to increase user satisfaction with these tools and reduce the cognitive attention required to use them. Furthermore, the evaluation of each of the improved implementations allows us to produce a list of guidelines to which future on-screen reading systems can adhere. These guidelines will aid in the creation of lightweight user-centered interfaces for digital reading.

There have been numerous academic studies that investigate the concept of digital reading and its applications. Princeton University [2009a], for example, recently performed a pilot study on eReading in a classroom setting. The voluntary project, which spanned a full university semester, studied 51 students using the Kindle DX to determine if eReaders could effectively reduce paper use without harming the overall classroom experience. The results showed that (at least for the students participating in the study) the use of eReaders significantly reduces the amount of printing performed by students. In fact, the average difference in paper use for students using the Kindle versus the control group (no eReaders) was as much as 55%. Princeton University as a whole, however, claims that since the inception of digital document delivery on campus, their printing use has actually *increased* [The Trustees of Princeton University, 2009b], a reality that has also been documented in other fields in recent years [The Economist, October 9, 2008].

This evidence points to a significant increase in digital document availability, coupled with a steady rise in paper usage. Although we might expect that this increased availability of digital documents would mean a decrease in paper use, in actuality the opposite is true, which suggests that many users print their downloaded digital documents. Since digital print-outs are expendable and easily replaced, many users will print several copies to distribute amongst others or to make notes on, exacerbating the already increasing use of paper. Clearly then, this 'print to read' [Marshall, 1997; Sellen and Harper, 2003] mentality is still a common occurrence despite the introduction of 'paper-like' reading screens, which causes skepticism about an office free from the printed page [Birkerts, 1994; Gass, November 1999; Gomez, 2009].

The reasoning behind the continued desire to print digital documents demonstrates a clear failure of on-screen reading and the tools designed to aid it. Surely, in a perfect world, reading and manipulating digital material would be almost indistinguishable from reading and interacting with paper—an ideal that could certainly bring the notion of the paperless office closer to reality.

Reading, the task central to the work presented in this book, is a complex and multi-faceted activity that takes years to master. For the majority of the time reading is not passive; instead it is performed in conjunction with other activities such as writing and highlighting [O'Hara and Sellen, 1997], or jumping non-linearly within a document [Marshall and Bly, 2005; O'Hara, 1996]. This concept can be referred to as *attentive* or *active* reading [Adler, 1940]. One of the early studies on the design of digital reading concluded that reading actually occurs in conjunction with writing over half of the time [Adler et al., 1998].

Performing active reading on screen is fraught with problems [O'Hara and Sellen, 1997], however, from hardware issues relating to screen size and resolution, to effective navigation and mark-up facilities. On some systems, trying to read more than one book at a time causes problems, and certainly makes it very easy to lose your place. While none of these problems are critical on their own, it is well-documented that both reading and active reading are easier [Adler et al., 1998; Hansen and Haas, 1988; Wästlund et al., 2008] and faster [Muter et al., 1982] to perform on paper than they are on screen. The main reason for this is that paper offers several advantages over computer screens including ease of annotation, navigation, and flexibility of spatial layout [O'Hara and Sellen, 1997].

The tangible properties of paper (e.g., it is light, thin, and flexible) afford many actions that are not possible with their digital equivalents [O'Hara, 1996; Sellen and Harper, 1997]. For example, paper can be folded, ripped, and stacked; it can be flicked, highlighted, and scribbled on, yet requires no batteries to function. Many researchers have studied affordance in the context of paper, both for investigative purposes and to aid in the production of more paper-like digital readers [Dillon, 1992; O'Hara and Sellen, 1997; Schilit et al., 1998a; Sellen and Harper, 1997]. The *New Yorker* magazine said, in 2002:

> "Digital documents, of course, have their own affordances. They can be easily searched, shared, stored, accessed remotely, and linked to other relevant material. But they lack the affordances that really matter to a group of people working together on a report."
>
> — *The New Yorker* [March 25, 2002]

The cognitive attention required to accomplish these tasks on paper is minimal, which often means that people will do it without thinking. For example, doodling on a piece of scrap paper then folding it inside a notebook can be done while in a lecture, an activity that does not usually break the user's attention out of the primary task of listening to the talk's content. In contrast, digital document manipulation is far less intuitive [Hansen and Haas, 1988] and consequently makes active reading tasks significantly more difficult.

The nostalgia of paper may also play a role in the skepticism surrounding the use of digital documents. Physical books are familiar, and after years of use often 'tell a story' about their inanimate life. Gass [November 1999] wrote an article about the pleasures of reading printed books, describing how the pages of his beloved copy of *Treasure Island* still bore the jam-stains from his childhood—a memory that now provides him with increased engagement with the book itself. In contrast of course, digital books do not age, and therefore do not contain any of the personal quirks that physical books acquire over their lifespan. Although there has been research into representing wear and tear on digital documents [Hill et al., 1992], for the most part, digital reading software maintains the pristine aesthetics of an eDocument throughout its entire existence.

Previous work on digital document manipulation has repeatedly demonstrated that poor human-computer interaction in digital reading inhibits user performance. For example, Marshall and Bly [2005] and O'Hara and Sellen [1997] have diagnosed several problems with reading and interacting with documents on screen, but do not posit any technical solutions. Other researchers such as Schilit et al. [1998a,b] propose solutions to specific problems within the digital reading world, but do not give any generalized improvements, suggesting that there is a clear gap in knowledge.

One approach to creating electronic documents that a variety of researchers have utilized is to follow the traditional book metaphor [Landoni and Gibb, 2000]. Traditional paper-based books are familiar, and there is speculation that maintaining the same model on screen improves users' interaction to the same information. In this context, readers are presented with a digital representation of a document that can be browsed and manipulated in a similar way to a paper book. Clearly, the physicality of paper is central [Luff et al., 2007; Sellen and Harper, 1997] to the way in which we interact with documents. The material value and 'heft' of the printed page undoubtedly contributes to its popularity, with one of the main objections to the eDocument being the plaintive "I could never curl up with a computer" remark.

A useful way of encapsulating the physical properties of paper is by 'lightweight navigation,' a term that describes actions that can be performed with little conscious effort [Marshall and Bly,

2005]. Although this term was originally coined to describe the affordances of paper, it is possible that it could also be applied to digital technology by probing which electronic properties might be able to be performed with a minimal amount of cognitive attention.

Given the overwhelmingly large increase in digital document uptake in recent years [BBC News, May 3, 2011; The New York Times, July 19, 2010], it seems timely to investigate the problems associated with electronic document manipulation tools in order to better understand and better inform future designs. Ideally, digital document software would allow users to annotate, manipulate, and interact seamlessly in a way that is minimally intrusive to the user, preferably by capturing the affordances of paper while at the same time transcending its limitations.

The term 'lightweight' and also its reverse, heavyweight, which describes actions that take a lot of conscious effort to perform, are central to the content of this book. By paying close attention to the lightweight properties seen in physical documents, digital document software can not only incorporate the physical affordances of paper, but also improve upon them by surpassing their limitations. With this in mind, our goal in this book is to prove by example that lightweight interaction is indeed possible on a digital level. From these examples it will then be possible for us to redefine the digital equivalent of the term to aid in future digital document designs.

1.1   OUTLINE OF THIS BOOK

This book starts with two chapters that introduce key concepts in reading. The first of these covers the history of reading, writing, and printing, and looks at how different generations of technology have been designed and created to support the needs of readers. The next chapter investigates several of the key concepts and reviews previous literature on the topic. We explore the history of reading and explain several analogies that neatly describe our goal of lightweight interaction for reading. We also describe the general literature on the topic of digital document navigation, to provide a broader context.

Instead of attempting to evaluate all lightweight attributes in a single integrated system, we have taken the approach of implementing multiple dedicated systems, each covering different, potentially lightweight features. Each of these implementations was engineered as a solution to problems identified with current digital document designs, and all were tested in user studies. We felt that constructing multiple systems, each offering its own contribution, allowed us to focus on specifics, and pin-point exact areas of interest.

Clearly, there are many potential areas that could have been explored to prove precisely which aspects of digital design could be considered lightweight. We have focused on two main areas of investigation:

1. Tools that are currently lightweight on paper but are heavyweight digitally;

2. Tools that are currently heavyweight on paper and are also heavyweight digitally.

Both these areas investigate tools that are currently considered heavyweight digitally, as our mission is to improve upon them by incorporating lightweight interaction into their design. We will accomplish this by first introducing concepts that are currently seen as lightweight on paper but are heavyweight digitally, which will allow us to assess whether mimicking paper practices will improve the usability of digital tools.

Although this is a useful first step, it is crucial to note at this point that printed documents are *not* a panacea—they also contain problems of their own which, in some situations, cause their associated tools to be heavyweight. By incorporating digital techniques in these cases, we attempt to overcome the problems of paper by introducing lightweight digital tools, in this case by investigating those that are heavyweight on paper and are also heavyweight digitally.

The first of our lightweight implementations is concerned with placeholding—a very common activity within printed documents but one that is poorly translated digitally. This section, then, is an example of a tool that is currently lightweight on paper but heavyweight digitally. We chose to investigate placeholders as a starting point for discovering lightweight attributes as it is one of a small set of functions that is commonly seen within digital reading systems, and one which we feel is relatively heavyweight in its current form.

During our investigation into placeholding, we made several notable discoveries, including the possibility that the space surrounding the document provides a useful area for additional contextual information. In our second investigation, we move on to substantiate this theory, by undertaking an in-depth, formative study into annotations in both their printed and digital forms. By first analyzing how and where placeholders are made on paper documents, we were able to implement a digital solution that mimics paper annotation practices in order to gain insight for our third investigation: a system that incorporates both placeholding and annotation into a single tool. In this final section we investigate the possibility of appropriation [Dix, 2007], a concept that is rarely seen in the digital world but is extremely common physically. We also explore the idea of a static digital workspace comparable to a desk or wall in the physical world, and the notion of direct manipulation for the creation and deletion of common objects.

As well as researching topics that are considered lightweight physically, we show that some areas that are considered heavyweight on paper can be improved on the digital level by incorporating electronic techniques. By doing so, we aim to determine some lightweight properties that are specific to digital document design and in turn prove that paper is not the perfect medium for active reading. In our final investigation, therefore, we investigate back-of-book indexing, a feature that is not particularly lightweight on either physical or digital documents. We chose to investigate the area of indexing as it demonstrates a clear example of an activity that can be significantly improved by incorporating ideas from the physical world with the computational power of a machine.

All of the implementations discussed above have been thoroughly tested by user studies, which have allowed us to gain real insights into the specifics of each system's features. Using the information gathered from our initial studies, we were better informed for the design of later systems, which eventually enabled us to lay down several lightweight attributes. This list of lightweight properties can then be used by designers as guidelines for the creation of new digital active reading software.

1.2   WHO SHOULD READ THIS BOOK?

If you are a critical reader and user of modern technology, and read books and other documents, you will enjoy this book. Better, if you are a programmer or developer, you will be able to take home lots of ideas for making reading technology better, more user-friendly, and, in fact, make it sell better. If you are an author, you will get lots of ideas about how to use margins and other features in books so that the active reader is better supported by your writing.

If you are a researcher, this book raises lots of ideas that can stimulate further research. The ideas in such a short book cannot be the final word; and in any case the technologies will push ahead—in this area a lot of research is trying to find out the scientific basis for what is or what will be commercially successful.

This book grew out of Jennifer Pearson's Ph.D. thesis. Other Ph.D. students may like to see how doctoral research transforms into a book.

While this book can be read with little technical knowledge, we do take a basic familiarity with the values, techniques, and methods of user-centered design for granted—we do not discuss in depth how user studies are run or analyzed, for example. To do further research in this exciting field the right research methods are essential so that we do not fool ourselves—when developing new technologies it is very easy to get really excited about them but not really know whether you *should* be excited. Many ventures fail because of this confusion! You may like to add Shneiderman and Plaisant [2004] and Norman [1988] to your active reading while you read our book …

CHAPTER 2

Reading Through the Ages

This chapter reviews the history of reading to demonstrate how changes in technology have influenced how people read, and show that how reading material is produced is a really interesting story. This history forms the backdrop for everything in the present book.

From the earliest marks on rocks and stone tablets to the current eReader devices, there have been centuries of change, and the introduction of different tools and techniques for helping the reader. Some of the inventions were deliberate and systematic, but tools have also emerged out of experience and chance. Most interesting is how reading styles, and active reading—the engagement of the reader with the written word—have developed with and driven the technological changes.

2.1 A BRIEF HISTORY OF READING

Reading is a millennia-old activity, which has progressed from being the preserve of an elite to, for many, a fundamental mark of civilization. In the first part of our review, we follow the changes that occurred to produce the current printed book. Alongside changes of production methods and materials, writers and editors regularly invented new techniques to help their reader better understand or find their way through the words in front of them. Figure 2.1 shows an overview of the main events in the development of reading.

2.1.1 SCRIBES AND SCHOLARS

In the earliest phases of human history, the only forms of reading and writing were drawings and pictographic forms on stones, cave walls, and other objects. It would appear from contemporary studies of pre-literate cultures in the modern world that at least some drawings represented externalized depictions of stories shared within a tribe or social group. Simple accounting information was similarly recorded on tally sticks, knotted cords, and other items, but again relied on the understanding and tacit knowledge of the 'reader.'

The earliest forms of what we would recognize as human writing emerged in Mesopotamia (modern Iraq and Iran) around 5,000 years ago (3,200bce). Writing appears to have primarily been adopted to support the work of the state—recording public affairs, administrative information, and legal decrees. More precisely, most writing that has survived was primarily for supporting the state. Perhaps there was just much more of it to start with!

Very primitive forms of 'text' or writing on objects such as sticks, bones, or hides and other early materials were perishable, and this means that very few examples have survived from these

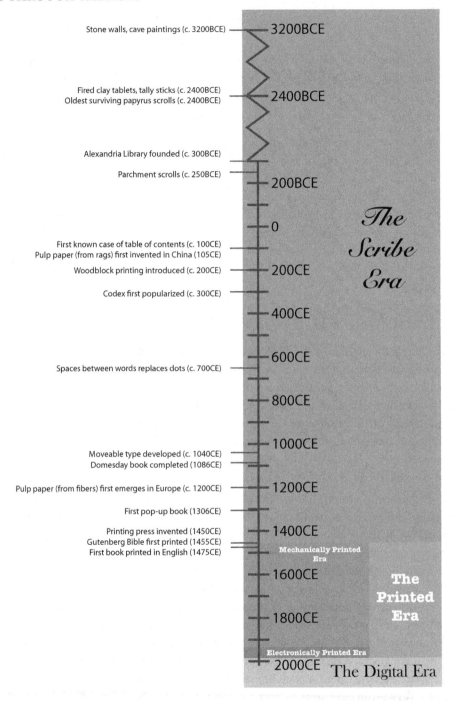

Figure 2.1: Reading through the ages *(Continues)*.

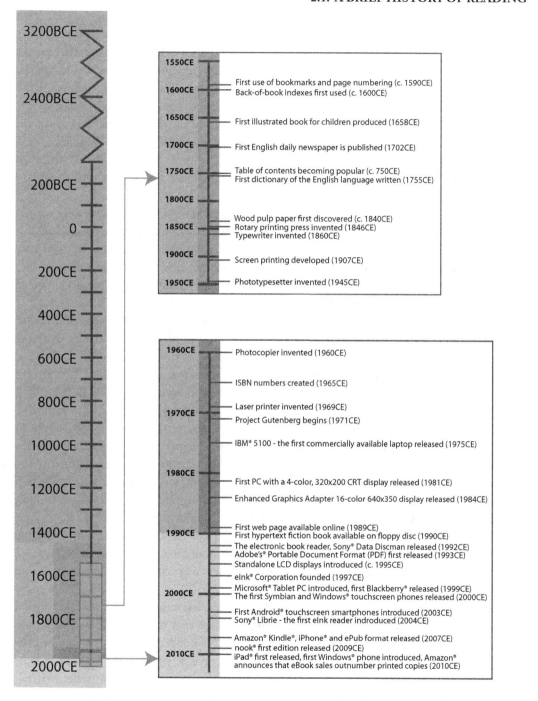

Figure 2.1: *(Continued)* Reading through the ages.

earliest periods. Harder and more durable materials better endured the millennia, so much of the earliest material we have today in any extensive volume is on stone or fired clay tablets.

The first major development in the technologies used for writing, which started to make the distribution of reading more widespread, was the adoption of papyrus in Ancient Egypt. For the first time, a major culture systematically adopted a writing form for much of its public life that was highly portable. The Egyptian interest in the afterlife, the deeds of their royalty, and other histories and myths meant that the storytelling that was the focus of pictographic records continued as a major part of the new form of writing. Egypt did also use animal hides for writing, as did other cultures. In fact, some Mesopotamian cultures used metal sheets. However, the relative ease with which papyrus could be produced in volume had a major impact on the growth of writing and reading.

Later cultures, including Greece and Rome, created and evolved their own writing systems, which included more abstract forms that owed more to the script-like writing of Cuneiform or Demotic text than the largely pictorial form of the hieroglyphs of Egypt. What was common across these new cultures, however, was that written text became more frequently used for communicating plays, poems, and stories than the official state purposes that were dominant in surviving formal hieroglyphs and other exclusive writing systems.

Egypt's library in Alexandria, a store of many texts, became a major hub of learning, and the copying of texts for transmission to other libraries and for private use—at least by the elite—became relatively commonplace.

Around the time of the 3rd century CE, a major transformation occurred. Previously, most 'books' were created and stored in rolls, in scroll form, but the codex now took over as the dominant form of book production and reading. The codex, paginated and bound like the print books of today, allowed much easier access to a specific point in the text, and was particularly useful for non-linear reading. As monks and scholars studied different parts of the Bible, or collections of plays or histories, the easier access of the codex provided a major advance in the ability to study and synthesize different parts of one volume. In some codices, we find the origins of the back-of-the-book index which is found at the rear of many textbooks today, and also the use of tabs (that is, markers), which are found in a variety of early reference documents.

The increasing availability of texts, even through the 'dark ages,' led to major changes in how people read. Many more people possessed small, individual collections of books, and the typical communal library grew in size and developed new ways of storing increasing numbers of books.

More dramatically, people started to read *silently*. Memoirs remark with surprise at the ability of some scholars to read while silent, though perhaps they were remarking that people were reading silently despite being *in the company of others*. It is not certain why this change occurred, but the change may have been influenced either by monastic preferences for silence generally, the problems of reading aloud in shared spaces, or simply a change in the way the written word was used socially. It may also have been because of cultural changes: perhaps reading silently was originally seen as subversive or occult. It is a fascinating area for historical and psychological research, but for us it is an example of where changes can occur in reading behavior without any obvious technological cause.

2.1.2 MECHANICAL PRINTING

Across much of the world, by the dawn of the 15th century, individual sheets of paper, and some smaller books, were printed from page-sized stamps that allowed the mass production of copies of an original image. The stamp was usually a solid wooden block, which was dipped in ink before being pressed to a page or piece of fabric. However, this method was very labor intensive and costly, and so was impracticable for many purposes.

Famously, Johannes Gutenberg radically changed the technology and economics of printing and reading by introducing movable type for mass production. This reduced the labor and cost of printing, and from its first use in around 1450, several major cultural revolutions ensued.

The concept of the book, it must be noted, is not an exclusively European invention, and printing elsewhere in the world did achieve high levels of sophistication. In fact, Chinese inventors had independently created movable type much earlier than Gutenberg. However, a number of technological, cultural, and economic factors mitigated against the diffusion of that method. The huge number of Chinese pictograms needed was greater than the relatively limited volume of letters found in European scripts, which increased the cost of each plate. Gutenberg's use of metal provided a critical mechanical difference in the ease of creating each original plate, and their lifespan, when compared to one made of ceramic, the material used in China. A third factor was the relatively low cost of many of the materials used, when compared to local prices for other goods.

In Korea, a metal moveable-type system had been created in the early 13th century, leading in 1392 to the establishment of a "Printing Office" for the imperial court. However, diffusion and uptake were slow, as the production and distribution of books was targeted at the socially elite. The technology only spread to nearby Japan when it was forcibly taken during an invasion of Korea, and prints then appeared for the first time in Japan around 1593, more than 350 years after the technology's inception.

In contrast, Gutenberg operated in a more commercial and mercantile context, with a wider readership. Due to his own success, and the establishment of effective competitors, publishing exploded as an industry. Three years before the Korean technique of printing arrived in Japan, Jesuits commenced printing in the country, using Gutenberg's methods, narrowly beating a neighboring technology that was some two hundred years older. While in Japan the Korean methods would become paramount for cultural reasons, elsewhere it was Gutenberg's technique, refined and adjusted over centuries, that would be adapted and continue in use to this day.

The basic mechanism introduced by Gutenberg endured for hundreds of years, albeit with many important and useful refinements in detail. It was only in 1846 that the rotary press was introduced, which substantially changed the physical design of the press and significantly accelerated the speed of printing. By 1893, refinements and adjustments were such that four different color plates could be used together to produce 'full color' printing, in a similar color principle to modern inkjet and laser printers. Screen printing was introduced for book printing in 1907, which improved potential resolution and, indeed, speed. Like many developments, the underlying technology had existed for a long time, in this case for approximately 200 years, but without being utilized or made practicable for publishing purposes. The movement to screen printing permitted the ready use of photographic stencils, which significantly improved the quality of detailed images.

In the twentieth century, various adjustments to the writing process, editing practices, and printing presses themselves allowed both the refinement of production and the increased availability of books at a price where leisure reading by laborers became viable. Indeed, in the depths of the 1930s recession, reading books from communal libraries was one of the few affordable pastimes for the unemployed.

2.1.3   ELECTRONIC PRINTING

The influence of electronic and electrical engineering slowly became stronger over time, but it was the arrival of the phototypeset process in 1945 that announced the first extensive use of electronics for determining the layout of books. Metal plate was replaced by photographic film, and images could be electronically scanned and transmitted long-distance, albeit slowly, often at low resolution, and at a high cost. The photocopier, which assembled scanning and printing into one device, appeared in 1960, followed in 1969 by the laser printer. Together, these different changes permitted cost-effective production of small volumes of books, and then, in the late 1980s, the emergence of desktop publishing as PC technology started to replace the dedicated phototypeset machine.

Fully electronic production became the norm, and was itself succeeded by digital editing, within 50 years. This rapid change was in sharp contrast with the 500 years over which mechanical printing had held sway. By 1995 almost all composition and layout was done electronically, with the film plates of phototypesetting remaining the norm for high-quality work.

Nonetheless, for the reader, the paperback book still represented a cheaper, more portable, and more usable form of book than the cumulative cost, fixed position and physical size of a desktop PC. Further changes were afoot, though, and by 1990, the first hypertext fiction had appeared in digital form. The Gutenberg Project started in 1971 to create digital versions of out-of-copyright texts, but only in August 1997 did it have 1,000 books in its catalog. The book in digital form was emerging, but only slowly and incrementally.

Another change was occurring almost imperceptibly, which would later have a major impact on the development of reading. While laptop computers did exist in the late 1980s, they had limited processing power, rudimentary displays (often lacking color), and poor battery life. While initially very expensive, they were the first steps toward making computer technology genuinely portable and widely available.

2.1.4 EVOLUTION FOR THE READER

After the introduction of the modern printed book, many elements for supporting the human reader's perusal of a text, that we now take for granted, would take decades or centuries to appear (or reappear). While reproduction of a single text was now simplified, personalized touches were now relatively more expensive, and the needs of a new, wider audience took time to develop and be discovered.

The first simple example is the bookmark. This is, nowadays, in its more aesthetic forms, either a separate leather strap or a fabric ribbon glued into the book's spine. The earliest surviving historic examples appear in the medieval period, before the paginated codex became predominant. Most of these early items are made either of parchment or of cord, and are permanently attached in some way to the book. The point of this marker was simply to keep the reader's position in the text, with minimal damage being done to the book. Given the price of books, leaving a folio open on its spine was to be avoided at all costs, as this weakened the expensive-to-repair binding.

For the modern codex, the first widespread adoption seems to have emerged in the 1590s, nearly 150 years after the first printed books. Many early bookmarks of this period were individually handmade, often by the reader, from simple materials. In the middle of the 19th century the increased availability of different materials led to the industrial production of aesthetic designs for purchase.

There are limitations to the individual bookmark. Used within a document, a single mark assumes only one place is of value to anyone, and this in turn suggests, if not requires, a linear style of reading. Books that are frequently used for reference to different points, such as pew Bibles in a church, are often provided with multiple bookmarks (usually fabric ribbons) to assist the reader.

Our second example of tools to assist the reader is the margin, something which is easy to miss. Margins in printed books were originally a product of the production process, but also enabled the pages to be handled without staining or spoiling the printed part of the page. Practically, smaller margins reduced the total cost of paper used in producing a book, so larger margins indicated expense and exclusivity.

Various practices for using the margins predated the printing press. Before printing emerged, scholarly manuscripts often included glosses and scholia—additional text placed near to the writing of the central document that explained and illuminated the main text. In some cases, especially with particularly esteemed works, the glosses were extensive, and became a significant part of the value of a specific book or scroll. These asides were produced personally and painstakingly by the scribe or scholar who wrote the individual copy of the text. In modern documents, a similar practice can be observed in scholarly editions of highly important works, such as Shakespeare's plays.

More commonly, corrections were often placed in the margin of a book after it had been created. This practice extended into the era of the printed book, given the high cost of the initial manufacture of the text.

Margins were also rapidly adopted for writing annotations and notes. When books were costly and rare, the addition of personalized handwritten notes was a hazardous affair, as it might reduce the value of an expensive object. In exceptional cases, where a specific copy was owned by an individual of particularly high reputation, this was not the case, but such examples are extremely rare.

As costs dropped and books became more commodified, the practice of personal annotations became more accepted and commonplace. By the middle of the 20th century, some school-books included blank areas for pupils to write answers to exercises and notes, inviting the use of the book by a single child over its lifetime. Before the creation of affordable paperbacks, this had been an unimaginable luxury.

Margins, therefore, evolved from places used to keep a book perfect to a personal space for notes. Their size and function varied in line with economic constraints and the purposes for which a book was printed. It is interesting how commodification plays an important role: if a manufacturer can make it seem useful to write answers into a book, then note-taking is promoted not just because it is useful for the individual reader but also because it effectively ruins the book for anybody else—so the manufacturer sells more copies.

Two final and interrelated examples of reader assistance are the back-of-the-book index and the table of contents. While these could be found, albeit created to a personal and idiosyncratic plan, in individual hand-written codices, these were previously personal items.

There are references to books written in the English language having an index from around the end of the 16th and beginning of the 17th century. One early example is found in Shakespeare:

> "... in such indexes, although small pricks to their subsequent volumes ..."
>
> — *Troilus and Cressida*

It is not clear whether this reference to an index is to a table of contents or to a modern type of index, though it is more likely to be the latter. Intriguingly, the first certain dates for the back-of-the-book index as such are of a similar date. The use of these techniques were rare. Alexander Cruden's Bible concordance of 1737 is believed by many to be the earliest index in an English book. One should bear in mind that alphabetizing the index (which seems obvious to us) was an idea that had to be invented too, and writing an index was so much work that it would hardly have been worth it until the printing press ensured that pagination was preserved from book to book—it is very unlikely that a scribe manually copying a book by hand would also want to redo the index as well!

In fact, even at the end of the 18th century, the back-of-the-book index was a rarity. Instead, detailed and complex tables of content with a series of descriptive phrases for each chapter were much more common well into the 19th century. Page numbers were only used for the chapter heading page, and not provided for the descriptive sentences that followed. The cause for this limitation was that an index could only be created after the main text was laid out and tabulated, which added extra delay and cost to production, and if new plates were created for a different page size, all the work had to be redone. Indeed, the cost of paper and ink was such that it was common for more popular documents to be printed on larger sizes for the gentry, and smaller pages for more ordinary folk.

Changes to technology meant that such factors were reduced, while the expertise needed to create indexes became more commonplace. Though these factors were small, their incremental effect was significant. The detailed back-of-the-book index assisted the reader to locate things even more rapidly than scanning through a chapter.

Page numbering itself emerged in the middle of the sixteenth century, some hundred years after the first printed book. With the first indexes emerging in approximately another fifty years, and a full index becoming common some three hundred years later, progress, while continuous, was also slow. These devices did not themselves require technological changes to be achieved, but their emergence demonstrates the ways in which the content of books was altered in response to the needs of readers. It is interesting how page numbering and indexing are separate ideas, each with their own history, and separately they are of limited use, but together they confer huge benefits to readers.

2.1.5   IMAGES AND FIGURES

The inclusion of figures in manuscript books (i.e., before print) was not inherently more complex than text. All parts were made by hand, and diagrams could be completed separately by an artist or by the scribe. There is a papyrus diagram in a geometry text by Euclid dating back to around 300CE, and conceivably copied from manuscripts dating back to Euclid himself, who lived 600 years earlier.

Figures were readily reproduced by wooden block printing or more simply by hand, and for creating full-page images, the arrival of the printed book brought little change. Many of the adjustments to print technology, in terms of materials and methods for impressing ink into the page, could be applied with equal ease to diagrams. The laborious setting of each written page was more readily mechanized and accelerated, whereas the expertise required to create good-quality figures remained similar, and even at times became more expensive. Hence, the relative cost of writing and images diverged, to the detriment of pictorial content.

Color of both writing and images was complex, but the closer one color was placed on the page to another, the more difficult the challenge became. So, this problem was more often an issue for figures or illustrations than for text. With changes of technology, high-quality line diagrams in color became more commonplace, most rapidly during the early 19th century. When photographic quality reproduction became possible in the 20th century, printing required specialist inks, high-quality paper, expert skills, and sophisticated equipment. It was only in the late 1960s and 1970s that the inclusion of high-quality color images became sufficiently affordable that image-rich 'coffee table' books became widely available.

Even today, for many books that include a few high-resolution color plates, these are included in specific parts of the book, grouped together. This is due to the economic and mechanical constraints of printing, and means that the images are often many pages distant from the text that relates to them. In turn, this has required the inclusion of a special part of the table of contents. The list of figures exists to help the reader locate where the diagrams or illustrations are that may be referred to in the text. It is interesting that some books (such as dissertations—books typeset by students rather than professionals) often retain a vestigial list of figures that serves no real benefit to the reader.

Clearly, computers allow us to have interactive books, but this is not a new idea. The English 18th-century landscape garden designer Capability Brown made use of flaps to illustrate 'before and after' views of his designs. We often think of such paper engineering as childish, but the audience for early 'interactive' books were adults, not children. It is believed that the first use of movable mechanics appeared in a manuscript for an astrological book in 1306. The Catalan mystic and poet Ramon Llull used a revolving disc or 'volvelle' to illustrate his theories. Throughout the centuries volvelles have been used for such diverse purposes as teaching anatomy, making astronomical predictions, creating secret codes, telling fortunes, and performing complicated mathematical calculations.

2.2   FROM PRINT TO DIGITAL READING

The arrival of the PC or (as it used to be called) the microcomputer had, initially, a more limited impact on reading than on publication. Though a lot of text was written on a computer, most was read from the conventional printed page.

Digital reading as such was starting to occur in the early 1980s, albeit most often for only shorter spans of text where the bother of printing was outweighed by the convenience of reading from the screen. Contemporary technology was primitive: most displays were monochromatic (amber, green, or white), while color monitors were as expensive as many of the more costly domestic personal computers. Resolutions were often as low as 640 × 480 pixels—now a resolution far below even the cheapest desktop, and surpassed by even today's mobile phones or small tablet devices. Color use was usually associated with resolutions of half that or less.

The visual presentation of contemporary texts was often rudimentary—establishing a common word-processor format took a decade, and the only common textual format was plain text, without any styling or embellishments. Distribution of digital content was physical, via floppy disk or, occasionally, tape. While digital reading was hailed as a future possibility, the low screen resolution, basic presentation, and costly distribution meant that reading on screen was, in practice, very limited.

From the first, primitive, devices, computer monitors increased their size and resolution, while color became a commonplace feature. By the mid-1990s, resolutions of 800 × 600 were becoming commonplace, but while the average PC had a better display, there was little change in the best available technology.

2.2.1 THE ERA OF DIGITAL PUBLICATION

By around 1995 the creation of documents was mostly performed on computers, while reading was done on paper. Digital content was still rare, and progress slow. A limited range of digital books was available, mostly in digital reproductions of older texts.

The initial use of digital formats for actual publication and dissemination had been held up by inconsistent and incompatible files, difficulty with rapid changes in software and content standards, and often a reliance on physical dissemination via floppy disk or tape. Digital documents had many of the limitations of printed books, with an inferior presentation and multiple difficulties in use. There were, and remain, concerns about protection of copyright. The photocopier had never fully threatened printing due to its high cost per page, but digital content was far too easily duplicated and distributed.

Despite these limitations and concerns, progress continued to be made toward digital publication, and hence the availability of digital books continued to increase. For example, Project Gutenberg progressed from 1,000 to 10,000 titles in six years—compared to 26 years for the first 1,000! What had caused this surge was the arrival of the Internet, which has in many ways been the root cause of much of the transformation of the publication, reading, and distribution of digital content.

2.2.2 HYPERTEXT AND ONLINE READING

Nowadays, the *hyperlink* is taken for granted as a technology for reading, being familiar to users from experience with web pages. But hyperlinks were a major revolution when first introduced. The first use of links can be traced back to the Stanford experiments of Doug Engelbart in the 1960s, but it was during the late 1980s that interest in the technology really took off, with the arrival of the mouse as an everyday component of computer hardware, and the gradual improvement of computer displays.

Improved screen size, resolution, and color meant that multiple views of a document could be displayed alongside each other, while the use of links broke longer documents into a series of fragments that might be viewed separately. These changes and new practices of use adjusted traditional understandings of reading. With distribution still relying on floppy disk or other physical media that would be considered inconvenient today, the spread of digital documents was slow and often tedious.

The emergence of the World Wide Web in the early 1990s brought a second, and critical, wave of adoption of hypertext. With the arrival of the Internet into everyday use, at least for a lucky few, digital reading became much more commonplace. This was driven by the radical change in the delivery of digital texts from physical media to electronic communication. In addition, the ongoing improvement of display technology made the physical demands of reading less pointed.

The web was driving the use of digital texts, and making delivery of digital documents much easier. Even into the 2000s, the web played two contrasting roles in reading. On the one hand, it made free or low-cost short documents readily available, and some publishers had experimented with it in a limited way for distribution. On the other hand, books were primarily being ordered through online stores and delivered via the post to the customer. Computers were now used for production and purchase, and for a lot of recreational reading … but further changes were afoot.

The appearance of affordable liquid crystal displays (LCDs), combined with improvements in battery technology and reduced energy consumption had an increasing impact on the form of computers. Laptops were becoming cheaper and lighter, and their displays were increasingly refined. These advances in the manufacture of computers were also creating new devices. Even before the year 2000, the mobile Internet was being mooted as a possibility, and mobile phones and other handheld devices were rapidly emerging as a future form factor for computing, and specifically for digital reading devices. The digital revolution was about to take a further step forward.

2.2.3   eREADERS AND eBOOKS

By the mid 2000s, the model of digital production and purchase, with reading in print, was well established. The physical, distribution, use, and space costs of paper now started to gather against its use. As an example, the Greenstone digital library was distributed in CD form, with one 5 inch disc containing thousands of books in electronic form in a medium that cost a few dollars per item. The space required for a single PC was much smaller than for the books themselves, and a whole library could be squeezed into the small box of a tower or laptop PC. The total cost of paper was much greater than for a CD, and while printing could be done locally, this would reduce some of the benefits of the digital medium, at least for the people who had to pay for the paper. Such incongruities started to fuel the demand for digital content, particularly, at first, for reference purposes. Encyclopedias contain a lot of short content, and therefore the digital form had fewer disadvantages than when reading a novel, where the whole story has to be read.

One popular early format for digital documents was the Portable Document Format (PDF). PDF was first intended as an easily transmittable printable file, allowing the easy distribution of content for printing. PDF was a derivative of the earlier PostScript language and format, which was used by many of the first computer-compatible laser printers. PDF, sometimes referred to as Acrobat, therefore traces its ancestry very closely to the later days of electronic printing, and focuses upon paginated documents and the ability to be printed onto pages with detailed control of both the position and appearance of content, because that is what printers require.

PDF was, and remains, a popular form for distributing truly digital content, and had the original advantage that it fitted directly into the existing digital work of the printing industry. An early rival to PDF was the Open eBook format, which was quickly succeeded by the ePub file format.

The ePub format, in contrast to PDF, is based on the HTML markup language used on the web, and has only relatively simple controls for the positioning and appearance of content. While often rendered in paginated form, underneath it draws more from the dynamic organization and presentation of web pages, and the 'page' itself has no permanent, enduring form. This has led to a number of problems which we will discuss later in this book.

While PDF and ePub formats allowed for the reading of content in digital form, ePub in particular is associated with a new and different device form factor.

One major development in the last few years has been the emergence of tablet PCs, such as the iPad, and eReading devices such as the Kindle. In each case, reading material has been provided in variants of the dominant PDF and ePub formats, particularly for paginated texts. Some manufacturer-specific formats also exist, though these are often derivatives of the ePub standard.

This new form of hardware follows research prototypes for lightweight, personal reading devices that can be traced back as far as the 1970s. Primitive commercial devices appeared in the early 1990s, such as Sony's Data Discman of 1992. The current forms draw from relatively new components, in particular the eInk display that is often used on eReader devices. eInk displays were pioneered by eInk Corporation, founded in 1997, and the first device was released in 2004, with Sony's Librie reader. eInk displays are, unlike LCD displays, not backlit, but reflect ambient light, just as traditional paper does. This makes them good to read in bright sunlight, where LCDs suffer badly. The technology is also very light and uses far less battery power than LCDs, as it only draws a charge when it changes the display. For this and other technical reasons, paginated text is the only practicable display method on devices that use the technology, because scrolling, which is typically used on the web, nullifies many of the advantages of eInk displays, particularly in terms of power consumption.

The popular Amazon Kindle was first sold in 2007, incorporating an eInk display, and has seen multiple releases, plus competition from Sony and other manufacturers. eInk displays now often include optional backlighting for low-light conditions, and the sharpness and contrast of the technology has advanced considerably. eInk devices are also relatively cheap to manufacture and purchase compared to other display technologies.

More recently, Apple has popularized the use of slate or tablet PCs with their iPad device, which uses a high-resolution LED type display (a close cousin to, and frequent replacement for, LCD technology)—but this draws power constantly, must be backlit, is heavier, and given processing, battery, and display costs, is considerably more expensive (in fact, costing around four times as much).

It is natural that hardware specifications will improve in coming years, and also that interaction design will be progressively improved. Other constraints such as what constitutes a portable size, and as a result, what viable input options can be included, will remain with us for some time.

While the early Kindle included a full keyboard, positional controls for highlighting text, for example, were very limited. As a result, once an annotation was being added, interaction was relatively easy, but selecting the right point was slow and laborious, due to primitive controls and the slow refresh speed of eInk displays.

More recent Kindle designs have, like Sony Reader devices and other competitors, abandoned the physical keyboard, in order to maximize the available screen space. This can in turn limit annotation facilities to simple bookmarks and other gestures that do not require textual input. While this design is sufficient for recreational reading, it fails to support more complex work-related reading. To mitigate this, many now use some form of touchscreen, but the types of touchscreen used are often only capable of quite coarse-grained mapping of where touches occur, and can struggle to support typing effectively.

In contrast, the iPad's quickly responding screen and more precise touchscreen keyboard combine to permit greater interactivity. Nonetheless, richer forms of reading can be hindered by the relatively clumsy text entry, and the backlit LCD screen is markedly more tiring, and often impossible to read in bright daylight.

Annotation facilities in such devices often retain the same interactive design as PDF reading software, which itself was originally intended to support proof reading and group editing of texts. Those specific tasks contrast with the emphasis found in most reading contexts, where the annotation tools take a secondary role to the task of reading.

The facilities of the ePub format are also less than ideal. Being built on a limited subset of the HTML markup language used in web pages, support for a number of established features of books is surprisingly weak. Large images, for example, cause particularly serious problems, being poorly or incompletely displayed, with little or no specific interaction.

In summary, existing digital document formats are far from ideal, and the hardware being built often supports casual reading much better than attentive, close interpretation of the text [Pearson et al., 2010].

2.2.4   DIGITAL RIGHTS MANAGEMENT

Originally, copying the written word was the hardest part of book reproduction. Gutenberg's printing press revolutionized everything, because reliable copying became trivial. Gutenberg effectively stands on the divide between the ancient world where the written text, scripture, was revered because it was so hard to copy and change and the modern world where copies of books are commonplace and active engagement with the word is encouraged. However, even for Gutenberg, the effort of setting up a book and printing it—typesetting—was very costly and out of the reach of ordinary people. As printing became established as an industry, the economics of scale exacerbated the differences: big publishers took over the 'means of production' and gained large markets out of the reach of individuals.

Then along came the PC. The new digital media are extremely easy to copy, and when combined with electronic reading facilities, effectively anyone with a PC or handheld connected to the Internet has the means of production and consumption in their own hands. Of course, this undermines the existing value system of centralized publishing, and the response was to introduce *digital rights management* or DRM. Some people rebrand DRM as *digital restrictions management*, and indeed there are two quite polarized views of it:

- Authors of material want to be paid for their work, and paid in proportion to their market contributions: a popular author feels they should be paid more than an unpopular author. Publishers invest in their printing processes and distribution channels, they pay authors royalties, and to stay in business they need returns on their investments. DRM can stop unauthorized copying, and can stop unlimited copying without paying the publishers. DRM allows many sorts of flexible approaches, such as the reader subscribing to documents rather than buying them outright and owning them—if a reader does not continue paying a subscription the book disappears. DRM opens up new ways of getting revenue, and preserving authority in original material.

- DRM allows publishers to impose restrictive practices on readers that will limit innovation. Conversely, as publishers upgrade their DRM technologies, existing approaches become obsolete, so older written material simply becomes inaccessible. Active readers who want to engage with the text are heavily restricted in what they can do. DRM restricts sharing information and, worse, seems to restrict it just when the technologies could have been developed to enable new things.

Such arguments will continue forever, and DRM is really beyond the scope of this book, except to note that active reading generally creates notes and marginalia that become part of the book being read. The question then is: who owns these notes? In fact, because of the scale of modern electronic reading, the notes themselves are less interesting than the fact that they have been made. If millions of people are commenting on a sentence in a book, that market interest may be more interesting to the publisher than what one individual is actually saying about it—this is the start of a new technological intersection between active reading and social media, again something we can be excited about, or depressed that DRM will tighten it up prematurely.

2.3 THE STATE OF THE ART

We now depart from the historic view of technology to examine the status quo today.

First, we look at the dominant 'visual book' metaphor. While scrolling views that take their form from standard computer interfaces do exist, there are a number of applications, for instance Apple's iBook app, that closely follow the appearance and the 'look and feel,' of familiar printed books.

Second, the presentation of the main text, whether the book metaphor is used or not, can follow a number of different styles. We examine the most common approaches to displaying the page, and again, see how different devices use one or more different layouts.

In the third part of this section we demonstrate how the book metaphor and different presentations combine in how contemporary book reading software communicates with its user and displays its content. By the end of this section, you will have a clear idea of some of the advantages and weaknesses we can expect to find in most of the reading software that you use day-to-day.

2.3.1   THE VISUAL BOOK METAPHOR

There are several mediums that have made the transition from physical to digital. When we think about how smoothly vinyl (music recordings made on plastic discs about a foot in diameter) shifted to CDs and eventually to MP3s, or physical film photographs to JPEGs or GIFs, it seems reasonable to question the migration of books and documents to the digital plane. One way in which documents can be represented digitally is by using the 'visual book metaphor,' a way of visualizing and interacting with digital text using typically physical techniques.

There has been a significant amount of research focusing on the visual book metaphor and its effect on digital document design. Landoni and Gibb [2000], for example, like many other researchers in the area, feel that a visual association with familiar concepts significantly aids the learning process. Their work, which focuses on the role of metaphors in digital document design, includes a study that investigated the importance of the visual book metaphor when presenting information on screen. The investigation used software that displayed a double-page spread to compare the effect of real books to the presentation of the same book electronically. The authors concluded that users found the representation was consistent with their mental model of a book and appreciated the enhanced functionalities the software provided. In a later work, Wilson and Landoni [2003] make several recommendations for effective eBook design including the adherence to certain aspects of the book metaphor (e.g., covers, indication of reading progress, and easy-to-use bookmarking and annotation) and the incorporation of hypertext (e.g., for table of contents and indexes).

Though there are many researchers (e.g., Crestani and Melucci [1998]) who believe, like Landoni, that embedding book metaphors such as indexes, tables of content, bookmarks, and so on, enhances digital versions of documents, there are also some who think that these are not necessary for ease of use. Nielsen [1990], for example, suggests that although readers are more likely to assimilate information faster when they encounter a familiar format (in this case, a paper-like book representation), future designs should in fact avoid implementing the book metaphor due to the limits it enforces upon conceptual models of search and non-linear navigation. In a later comment, Nielsen stated that

"... the book is too strong a metaphor."   — Nielsen [July 26, 1998]

as it tends to lead designers away from the potential of new media capabilities, thus meeting with the functions of paper but never actually surpassing them.

The idea of exceeding the limitations of paper by applying digital techniques was also touched upon by Shneiderman and Plaisant [2004] in their book *Designing the User Interface*, where they discuss the concept of on-line manuals:

"... the designers will be most effective if they can redesign the manuals to fit the electronic
medium and to take advantage of multiple windows, text highlighting, color ..."

— Shneiderman and Plaisant [2004]

and:

"... a close match between printed and online manuals can be useful."

— Shneiderman and Plaisant [2004]

This suggests that combining elements from the physical world with digital enhancements will improve the interaction with digital reading systems. The work presented in this book focuses very much on the concept of the book metaphor by combining lightweight techniques seen in the physical world with purely electronic enhancements in an attempt to improve the overall interaction design of digital reading systems.

2.3.2 PAGE DISPLAY

One important aspect of digital document representation is the way in which the text is displayed—particularly when considering the visual book metaphor. Pagination is the process of dividing documents into discrete pages for display.

pag-i-na-tion (*noun*) A sequence of numbers or signatures assigned to pages in a book, periodical, etc. Also: The action of marking the pages of a book or other written text with such a sequence.

Before the age of computers and digital texts, the main purpose of pagination was to indicate the correct order of content within a document and to facilitate easy referencing to specific points within the text. Page breaks on physical documents occur naturally either when the end of a page is reached or when the editor feels a new page is appropriate (e.g., at the end of a chapter, or to avoid orphaned lines, for example). With the exception of ancient scroll parchments (where pagination was not necessary), all modern physical books include pages.

Digital documents are not bound to the physical page and can therefore be split anywhere depending upon where and how they are being displayed. Many web-based applications (e.g., search page results or forum threads) will display a specific number of lines before a break, whereas smaller screen reading devices alter the page breaks depending upon the size of the text. Alternatively, one may choose not to paginate text at all, leaving reams of continuous text on the same 'page,' and using scroll-bars for navigation as opposed to the common 'next' and 'previous' links, or swiping gestures.

Some of the more common types of pagination used in digital document readers are described below:

Single Page Display: Only *one* page is displayed on the screen at a time. The 'next' and 'prev' buttons change the view to the next or previous page. An example is shown in Figure 2.2(a).

Single Page Continuous Display: Displays every page of the document one directly after another on the screen. Controlled via the scroll-bar for continuous navigation, or the 'next' and 'prev' buttons to skip to the start of a page. This option facilitates uninterrupted reading as it can display the top of a page at the same time as displaying the bottom of the previous page. An example is shown in Figure 2.2(b).

Double Page Display: A *double page spread* (two adjacent document pages) is displayed on the screen at a time. As with the single page display, the 'next' and 'prev' buttons are used to change the currently open pages. An example is shown in Figure 2.2(c).

Double Page Continuous Display: Identical in behavior to the single page continuous display, except that instead of a single page it displays a double page spread. An example is shown in Figure 2.2(d).

No Pagination: Text content is *not* paginated at all; scroll-bars are used to progress linearly through the document and hyperlinks are utilized to skip to specific points within the text. An example is shown in Figure 2.2(e).

The user interfaces described throughout this book make use of several of these pagination methods, depending upon the function of the system in which they are included.

2.3.3 REALISTIC BOOK SOFTWARE

Given the widely recognized advantages of printed media, some researchers have tried to reproduce the experience of physical books as literally as possible when using digital texts, which allows the direct transfer of behaviors between the two mediums. Different approaches have been taken within this general paradigm that attempt to bridge this platform gap, often by incorporating graphical representations of physical book behavior into digital document reader design. These types of realistic document implementations have a strong relationship with the visual book metaphor.

One of the earliest projects on the topic of realistic book representations was the British Library's 'Turning the Pages' project [British Library, 1997]—a virtual software environment for reading scanned documents in a realistic paper-like manner. The software, which has been designed for use on a touch-screen interface, shows a double page spread of what resembles a physical book sitting on a desk. The book itself appears to be three-dimensional and pages can be turned by swiping a finger across the touchscreen.

The 'Turning the Pages' project inspired early work on realistic digital page turning. The book metaphor, and the graphical page modeling described by Chu et al. [2003], was a foundation for what they later describe as 'realistic electronic books' [Chu et al., 2004], a concept that allows users to interact with physical book visualizations of text-based documents within a digital library. The design of the realistic book system imitates paper in several ways previously unexplored by digital document designers, including: a double page spread, pages curling as the user navigates between them, bookmarks protruding the closed page leaves, and applying aging processes to heavily viewed pages.

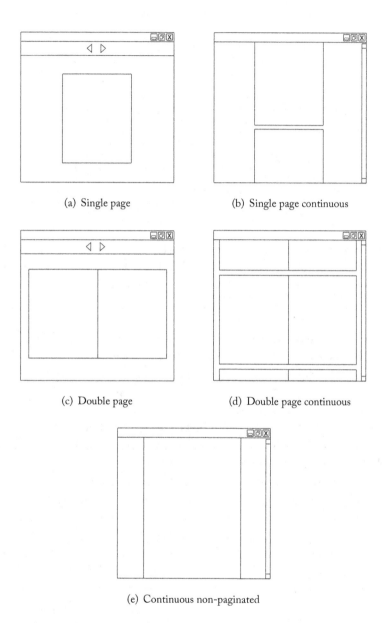

(a) Single page   (b) Single page continuous

(c) Double page   (d) Double page continuous

(e) Continuous non-paginated

Figure 2.2: Examples of five popular ways of paginating digital documents.

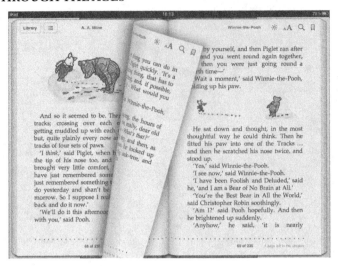

Figure 2.3: A screen shot of page turning on the iPad iBooks app—the user's finger 'holding' the page corner is not visible in this picture! Interestingly, the picture looks very static, yet the whole point of the page turning visualization is to be, and to feel, very interactive.

Other researchers have also attempted to create graphical three-dimensional representations of physical books. Card et al. [2004] implemented a system called 3Book which was designed with the intention of rendering indefinitely large books at interactive speed levels. The interface, which is similar to the realistic book implementations, supports activities such as bookmarking, text extraction, and on-the-fly indexes.

Portable computing devices such as tablets and smart phones are now attempting to replicate the book metaphor in their software. Applications such as iBooks and Stanza provide 'paper-like' page curling or turning by means of finger swipes across touchscreen displays (see Figure 2.3). Despite the familiarity of these types of interfaces, they still suffer from some serious usability issues which could hinder the digital active reading process, suggesting that there is still work to be done in the area.

The turning of the page, for example, while aesthetically pleasing, is not necessarily a positive contribution to usability. The response speed of programs such as these, due to the computational cost of rendering page turning in detail, is often poor. Furthermore, the ability to slowly 'curl' digital pages is typically incomplete as, in the majority of cases, only one page can be turned at a time. In contrast, on-paper users can curl multiple pages at once, allowing fast flicking through a document as well as the ability to quickly switch between two non-adjacent pages.

Prior research conducted on realistic electronic books provides a grounding for the work presented in this book. Although for the most part our implementations do not religiously follow the book metaphor (that is, all but one of our interfaces use single-sided display as opposed to

double page spread), we do make a direct comparison to a physical book in our largest investigation into note-taking. Instead of slavishly duplicating every aspect of the physical book in
our design, however, we cautiously trim what we argue are inappropriate migrations from the
physical interaction. For example, as we mentioned above, the visual curling of pages within an
electronic document, despite its clear familiarity, does not translate well to the digital plane due
to restrictions placed upon its functionality, as well as problems resulting from page rendering
[Hong et al., 2005].

We cannot force physical metaphors into digital book design, but we should pick out useful
aspects that transfer in a meaningful and practical way. Just because a property can be considered lightweight physically does not necessarily mean its digital equivalent will also prove to be
lightweight [Heim, 2007].

2.3.4   THE AFFORDANCES OF PAPER PROJECT

The 'Affordances of Paper' project [O'Hara, 1996] was pursued in the mid 1990s with the aim to
understand the persistence of paper in the workplace by analyzing how the physical properties of
paper support human work and interaction.

Reading is not a stand-alone activity; there are a diverse range of reading strategies as well as
navigational and manipulation issues that can be applied to a wide collection of reading activities.
One of the key goals of the project was to characterize how reading strategies are influenced by
the goals and motivations of the reader and to consequently develop a framework to understand
the interactive properties of paper. The heart of this investigation is the concept of affordance,
paying particular attention to the understanding of how paper's affordances support the task of
reading and comprehending documents. This understanding was achieved by comparing these
paper-based affordances with the affordances of digital document readers for the same class of
reading tasks. The resultant typology shows how the different reading strategies adopted by users
enforce a set of demands upon the properties required of the reading medium.

The physical properties of paper mean that it generally supports these demands without
significant effort from the user. The authors suggest that although emerging digital technologies
make some progress toward meeting these demands, they do still suffer problems. One of the
major points to take from this study is the demands required of the medium in which a document
is presented: in our case, electronic. Tying this in with the notion of primary and secondary tasks
(see Section 3.1.1) and the active reading process, the first demand is vital to the work presented
in this book:

> "... the ability to make notes on and annotate a document in a way which allows integration with
> the primary task of reading and comprehension ..."   — O'Hara [1996]

This point confirms the importance of making digital mark-up tools lightweight to allow maximum cognitive attention to be paid to the primary task of reading and comprehension.

2.3.5   AUGMENTED READING HARDWARE

Another way in which the book metaphor has been explored by researchers over the last few years is through augmented reading appliances. One of the principal works on the topic of digital reading appliances is the XLibris project [Schilit et al., 1998a], which focuses heavily on augmented hardware that imitates paper. The project's main aim is concerned with the process of active reading outside of the desktop PC and the impact of both physical form and interaction on the overall reading experience. To achieve these goals, they create the 'active reading machine'—a pen-based tablet display that uses the 'paper document metaphor' to support the analytic reading of digital documents. By using a modified tablet PC that includes pressure strips and animations for page turning and free form digital ink for annotations, the XLibris system is able to support paper-like tangibility from an entirely digital device.

Another, more recent, attempt at providing a 'book-like' hardware platform, this time making use of multi-touch displays as opposed to the single touch tablets used by XLibris, is Liquid-Text [Tashman and Edwards, 2011b]. LiquidText has been designed to support the digital active reading process by incorporating a flexible digital document representation that is controlled via gestures on a multi-touch screen. Unlike the work we present in this book, where we aim to migrate some of the lightweight properties of paper to the digital level, the LiquidText interface does not attempt to replicate the affordances of paper. Rather, it tries to surpass their limitations by facilitating a more fluid digital solution with a high degree-of-freedom to annotate and reorganize documents.

The touch-screen nature of the LiquidText hardware allows users to interact with multiple objects at once to provide a rich set of gesture-based interaction techniques for the digital document representation. The interface itself offers a non-paginated display which is collapsible to allow users to simultaneously view multiple parts of the document at once, an issue associated with digital documents that has previously been described as problematic [O'Hara, 1996]. Clearly, the use of non-paginated displays differs considerably from the paginated structure of the physical book, which can cause problems when attempting to replicate some of the lightweight properties of paper. For example, what we know as bookmarks would be obsolete in such a display as there are no 'pages' to mark; instead markers must be made on specific parts of the text. The work we present in this book, therefore, does not make use of non-paginated displays like LiquidText as our research is concerned with taking the physical book metaphor and refining and enhancing its features in order to create digitally lightweight interactions for active reading systems.

Another recent development in single display reading hardware is by Chen et al. [2011] who have also utilized the slate PC form-factor in their implementation, PageSpark. As with the LiquidText system, the hardware used for the PageSpark interface is off-the-shelf (in this case an iPad) as opposed to the modified technology used by XLibris. The main goal of PageSpark is to enhance traditional static magazine content by creating interactive multimedia applications that run on devices that are close in size and resolution to physical books. One of the most relevant features of the PageSpark system is the page elements interaction that allows independent single column scrolling within multi-columned documents. This technique is a good example of how designers are making better use of digital technologies to enhance digital reading—a trend that we follow closely in all the systems described in this book; as opposed to blindly following the conventions set by the physical page.

2.4   FUTURE DEVELOPMENTS

As the uptake of digital reading technology progresses, some changes to technology and patterns of behavior are foreseeable.

Basic eReaders increasingly use touch-based input, regardless of whether they use eInk or LCD displays. Changes in touchscreen technology are underway. At present, touch pressure is not distinguished, and the technology cannot necessarily discriminate between touches by different objects. In future, it is likely that touches by finger and, say, stylus will readily be distinguished, as well as different pressures. This will radically expand the range of designs that can be built (e.g., at present resting your hand on a screen to write with a stylus causes problems—this could be avoided in future).

Display technology is also improving. eInk color displays are under development, and alternative forms of LCD technology can provide colored displays that are readable in bright daylight. This will permit reading of color documents in a wider variety of lighting conditions, but also facilitate a much richer range of annotation and other interactions than a black-and-white display ever can.

Beyond incremental improvements, physical interaction sensors that are currently only available on desktop PCs and game devices, such as the Microsoft Kinect, will likely appear as supplementary input technologies. For example, swiping in front of a screen, rather than touching on it directly, will be able to act as a command. Some initial tablet PCs can achieve this (poorly) at present using a video camera, but future technologies will permit a clearer distinction between commands, and a richer range of gestures and controls.

The impact of these changes does need to be kept in context. At present, the main shortcomings of previous devices, such as display quality, have been overcome, and this has improved the usability of basic, linear reading. While input techniques are certainly a current constraint, they are not in themselves a direct impediment to fulfilling the needs of someone who needs to analyze a text with close scrutiny. Rather, it is the balance and form of the interaction design that impedes the serious reader. Therefore, while more exotic and complex interaction technologies may assist us to achieve that goal, the deeper consideration of users' tasks, goals, and requirements is more likely to lead to tangible benefits.

The development of reading has never been driven by technology alone but also by changes in society and individual behavior. Some prospects of societal and behavioral change may already have been glimpsed.

There are numerous informal pieces of evidence, in YouTube videos and blog sites, for example, that demonstrate the rapid familiarization of infants with the swipe gesturing of touchscreen devices. For many of us today, the response and interaction of paper are dominant. In that context, the current 'realistic' approach of treating and presenting digital documents in a way similar to paper books allows the transfer of familiar skills. This may no longer apply when today's infants are, say, thirty years old. It is too early to prejudge potential impacts, but some change is likely.

A different issue is annotation which, once a permanent despoiling of a single copy, is now, at least potentially, transferable to other copies, and easily made invisible. It is, therefore, both more durable and less permanent. Furthermore, annotations can be indexed and linked in ways completely impossible on paper.

One predictable opportunity will be the rise of multiple devices (e.g., Chen et al. [2012]; Pearson et al. [2012a]). It is easy to imagine that the current economics of reading devices are permanent. They are unlikely to be. Affordable current PCs are the same price (in raw numbers) as microcomputers of thirty years ago. In terms of affordability, this is a huge price reduction, and the leap in sophistication is striking. The needs of basic reading devices may well not leap so quickly, but today's basic Kindle is a mere $69, and likely to get cheaper in real terms in the future. Having several such devices in one household or even owned by one person is not only reasonable, but in fact a reality for some already. How to exploit this opportunity well is a genuine and unanswered question.

There are tangible barriers too. The use of within-document search (or 'Ctrl-F') is little used by many, and lacks many of the subtleties of a dedicated index. The skillful human indexer can include implicit and non-literal similes for a word that the letter-for-letter matching of within-document search lacks. Conversely, the traditional back-of-the-book index requires repeated turning of pages and difficult gestures, and it also prejudges which words the reader may search for. Neither the old nor the new alone is ideal.

How to blend both the advantages of the old with the opportunities of the new is a recurring problem in the history of reading. Repeatedly, when technologies have changed, best practices of the old ways were abandoned in the adjustment to new methods. All too often, the neglected techniques were later reintroduced to solve, again, problems the magic of new technology ultimately did not eliminate, and needs that the transition pushed temporarily back in order to mitigate the costs of change.

In the digital domain the opportunity for functionality is limited not just to the publisher and author, but also to users, developers of reader software, librarians, and others. The door to the future is open, and we will cross through it. The question is, in what manner will we, as a technological society, take our next step forward?

This book aims to make a lasting and useful contribution to the future of digital reading. Reading is the commonplace and critical task of the 'information society,' and will very likely remain so. We tease out enduring concepts that can explain the successes—and failures—of the past and, looking forward, be applied to designing novel and improved interactions for reading.

2.5 SUMMARY

King Mindon, who founded the last capital of Burma, Mandalay, wanted to leave a book for posterity, and in 1860 he started its construction. His book, a copy of the Pali Canon of Buddhist scripture, which dates back to 30BCE, and in oral traditions to much earlier times, was finished in 1868. The book consisted of 1,460 stone pages, weighing over 400 tonnes altogether. The whole book was housed in the Kuthodaw Pagoda, which consisted of 729 separate stupa that housed the Canon's tablets. Within twenty years, the British invaded and ransacked the book, stealing its decorative gems and gold lettering. Fortunately, the Kuthadow Pagoda has now been restored, and is one of the wonders of the world. In terms of posterity, the span of 250 years to today is not long, and yet King Mindon's efforts already seem unwieldy and quirky, not least because the immovable book does not support any form of active reading! So, we are led to ask, what will contemporary books, printed or digital, look like in a small fraction of that time, when all ideas now go from essential to obsolete in a few years?

This chapter has provided a glimpse into the processes of change that have produced reading technologies as they stand today. Each time that a new medium has superseded the previous one, there has been a tendency for the best existing practices for supporting readers to be lost. Each supporting tool requires time for the authors and editors (in the case of print) and developers (for digital documents) to catch up. To know which practices to sustain we need first to better understand in more detail how reading actually works.

CHAPTER 3

Key Concepts

This chapter reviews a range of research that illuminates what is actually happening when someone reads. Reading is a skill that takes decades to master, and is strongly influenced by the context in which it occurs. While, like riding a bicycle, reading is a skill we can take for granted once mastered, in fact the picture underneath is highly complex. The complexity of reading is suggested by the effort that is expended by us all to learn how to master it. A better understanding of what is happening when we read, and how we are affected by our interactions during reading, will help us appreciate why specific techniques are effective (or not), and help us design and plan better interactions.

3.1 READING

3.1.1 ACTIVE READING

Reading is rarely passive. For many, the act of reading is usually accompanied by thinking and learning, which often leads to other activities such as note-taking, highlighting, and underlining [O'Hara, 1996]. This process is known as *active reading* and was first defined by Mortimer Adler in the 1940 edition of *How to Read a Book* [Adler, 1940]. Active reading is a common activity for those who engage in knowledge-based tasks [Adler et al., 1998], particularly when in the workplace. Even those who read books for fun may also engage in the active reading process, perhaps by making a list of characters within a novel or writing down words they wish to define later.

Active reading is a pervasive theme throughout this book. The tools we implement in subsequent chapters have been designed specifically to aid in the process, and do so in a way which is minimally disruptive to the primary task. In this context, the primary task will be the active reading task; that is, thinking and engaging with the text. Secondary tasks involve any other activity. For example, when marking up a document, the primary task of the user will be reading the text and thinking about how to annotate it; the secondary task will be physically picking up a pen and writing notes on the page. For a user to be fully engaged with the primary task, it is beneficial for the secondary tasks to be as minimally cognitively demanding as possible to ensure the maximum amount of attention is being left for reading.

3.1.2   READING IN CONJUNCTION WITH WRITING

One of the early studies on work-related reading habits [Adler et al., 1998] confirmed that in the majority of cases, reading occurs in conjunction with writing—with eight out of 15 subjects performing the action between 75% and 91% of the time. This investigation also confirmed that there are many different *purposes* for reading. Some examples include: reading to remind, reading to answer questions, reading to learn, reading for cross-reference, and reading to support discussion.

This data concurs with the work of O'Hara [1996] and confirms that there are many types of reading other than simply to read for information. Many of the purposes of reading involve reading in conjunction with writing. Clearly, the process of writing is a complex activity within the work-related reading process, and one which has many purposes. It is, therefore, vital to the success of any digital active reading interface that the tools designed to aid in this process are as universal and easy to use as possible to ensure these goals are effectively achieved.

In addition to the different reasons one might write while reading, Adler et al. [1998] also describe a taxonomy for five different categories of writing used in their analysis:

Creation: Creating a new document or editing an existing document.

Note-Taking: The writing of abbreviated or unstructured text used primarily as a temporary way of jotting down ideas before the writing of a final finished document.

Annotation: Writing on an existing document about the text within it. Annotations usually contain markers to their surrounding document content.

Form-Filling: Filling in structured forms or writing in a pre-defined and prescribed manner, e.g., filling out an application form.

Updating: Updating calendars or schedules.

Here, Adler et al. take the term *note-taking* to be the unstructured comments made before embarking on writing a larger document. In this context, then, note-taking is separated from the term *annotation*, which they take to mean the informal markings made upon pre-existing literature. In this book, we too will be separating these terms, investigating the topic of annotation, which discusses mark-ups made on top of pre-made documents, and note-taking, which in our case refers to the process of making notes on and around documents using digital sticky notes.

Although active reading covers a diverse range of activities, the process of reading in conjunction with writing forms a large portion of a user's engagement with a document, and one which we will be following closely throughout several of the investigations we discuss in this book. One topic that is central to all the work presented here, however, is the concept of on-screen reading, an activity that is integral to any digital active reading system.

3.1.3   ON-SCREEN READING

The main focus of this book is to improve the active reading process on digital documents, which, of course, relies heavily on reading from computer screens. There have been a host of studies that have investigated on-screen reading. Back in the early 80s, Muter et al. [1982] performed a study asking 32 participants to read continuous text for two hours, half of them reading from a video screen and the other half reading from a printed book. Although they concluded that there was no significant difference between the comprehension or subjective measures of discomfort (i.e., dizziness, fatigue, or eye-strain), the results showed that the participants read 28% more slowly on video screens than from physical books. A follow-up study conducted in the same manner was undertaken by Krunk and Muter [1984] to investigate the reasons behind this difference in speed. Their results suggested that the formatting (i.e., the number of characters and lines per page) and interline spacing were the main reasons for the difference in speed between the two mediums as opposed to the contrast ratio or rendering time. Although this research may seem somewhat archaic, having been performed on monochrome CRT monitors, the principle of the study results remains valid, particularly when applied to small-screen devices such as eReaders where the formatting of text is periodically changed.

The view that text size and formatting hinder the on-screen reading process is also shared by Mills and Weldon [1987], and after an extensive review of empirical studies regarding the readability of text from computer screens, they argue that

> "Paper appears easier and faster to read than computer screens, but the size of the effect depends on the quality of both the paper and screen presentation."
>
> — Mills and Weldon [1987]

Hansen and Haas [1988] conducted a series of experiments in an attempt to explain the differences in performance between the two media, identifying seven factors that could contribute. The results of four experiments conducted to evaluate these differences, including page size, legibility, responsiveness, and tangibility, all confirmed that paper was better than computers for reading in every condition.

In the early 90s, Dillon [1992] produced an extensive review of the literature relating to on-screen reading, and evaluated the reading process in terms of speed, accuracy, fatigue, comprehension, and performance. In terms of speed, Dillon concurs with previous works and suggests that there is a performance deficit of between 20% and 30% when reading from screen as opposed to reading on paper.

In terms of subjective preference, the majority of the literature (e.g., Adler et al. [1998]; Hansen and Haas [1988]; O'Hara and Sellen [1997]) suggests that paper is the favored medium for reading—a trait that is even more prominent when considering reading in conjunction with writing. There have been many studies that have focused on user behavior while reading and writing on screen. Adler et al. [1998], for example, discussed the differences between paper and on-screen active reading and concluded that paper-based reading and writing accounted for 85% of people's total activity time, whereas on screen reading and writing accounted for only 13%.

These results were even more surprising, as the authors found that the participants all had at least some essential data stored on their computers which required them to use them for at least some portion of their work. This suggests that paper is a considerably more popular alternative to reading and writing on screen even in situations where a vital part of the task involves computers. The authors justify the choice of paper over an on-screen alternative, at least in some situations because:

> "… paper supports their particular reading and writing tasks better, and that the on-line alternatives simply fail to provide the critical affordances of paper."   — Adler et al. [1998]

The effect these paper affordances have on the active reading process is seen in many aspects of digital document interaction. O'Hara and Sellen [1997], for example, state that

> "Annotation on paper was relatively effortless and smoothly integrated with reading compared to on-line annotation which was cumbersome and detracted from the reading task."
>   — O'Hara and Sellen [1997]

The tangibility that paper affords is a common theme in the reasoning behind the poor performance of on screen reading and writing, and results in a high proportion of users printing digital documents to mark them up. Marshall [2009] commented that there were occasions when even environmentally mindful users would print documents:

> "Even the most environmentally conscientious reader turns to the printer when asked to review a journal submission, to proofread a document, or to refer to the document in situations that a laptop (or even a portable reading device) would be awkward."   — Marshall [2009]

Sellen and Harper [1997] suggest that there are good reasons for the continuing use of paper in organizational life, and attempt to justify the low uptake of on-line reading and writing as well as the 'print to read' mentality of many users by stating that:

> "The critical differences have to do with the major advantages that paper offers in supporting annotation while reading, quick navigation, and flexibility of spatial layout. We found that these, in turn, allow readers to deepen their comprehension of the text, extract a sense of its structure, create a writing plan, cross-refer to other documents, and interleave reading and writing."
>   — Sellen and Harper [1997]

3.1.4   READING AND COGNITION

Mayes et al. [2001] conducted experiments to determine if reading information on screen resulted in poorer performance than that of paper. As with the work of Dillon [1992], the categories used to determine performance within their studies were classified as: reading time, comprehension of the text, and mental workload. The first of their two-study analyses concluded that although there were no significant differences between mental workload and comprehension, those who read on screen took considerably longer to complete the reading tasks than those who were reading from paper. Realizing this, the authors then conducted a second study in order to determine if an increase in demands on working memory was responsible for these performance detriments.

To investigate these issues, Mayes et al. introduce the term *secondary tasks*, which can reveal when a user's limited working memory capacity is exceeded (the study used the memorization of a list of letters as an example). They argue that if reading from a screen increases workload due to the burden of additional cognitive demands of the task, then users will be less able to store secondary task information. Thus, in theory, those who are reading from a screen will exhibit lower performance on later recall of the secondary task information than those who read from paper.

Although their first study concurred with the work of Muter et al. [1982] that reading is faster to perform on paper than it is on screen, the results from their second study, where secondary tasks were introduced, indicated that people can in fact read from screens as fast as they can on paper. They suggest however, that when the secondary task requires attention from the user, those who are reading from paper tended to recall information better than those who read from a screen. They conclude from this that performance, at least in terms of information comprehension, is negatively affected by on-screen presentation.

The suggestion that reading from a computer screen reduces the working memory capacity for reading has been further investigated by Wästlund et al. [2005] who conducted studies that avoid any confounding page layout variables such as line length, fonts, and kerning. The main findings of this experiment were that reading comprehension is more difficult and mental work-load higher when performed on-screen than when performed on paper. They therefore conclude that reading on screen reduces the working memory capacity by reallocating cognitive resources to document navigation.

This evidence suggests that the process of actually interacting with the computer is the cause of this performance deficit. In a later paper, Wästlund et al. [2008] describe the navigation of on-screen reading to be part of the reader's overall processing capacity:

> "Reading on a computer screen involves both the process of reading the presented text and handling the computer, thereby, while reading a document onscreen, the reader's processing capacity is being utilized not only for decoding but also for page navigation."
>
> — Wästlund et al. [2005]

It is clear from the literature that the cognitive workload required to read on screen is higher than that of paper, thus suggesting that the process of interacting and navigating with the document using the computer is hindering the on-screen reading process. In terms of active reading, this statistic is likely magnified. By introducing another cognitive process into the equation (i.e., writing, highlighting, underlining, etc.), the user has more actions to perform interactively using the computer, a process likely to utilize additional processing capacity. It is vital to the success of any active reading software, then, that the cognitive workload required to use the tools is as low as possible to leave more processing capacity for the primary active reading task.

3.2   LIGHTWEIGHT INTERACTION

The physical properties of paper afford many actions that are difficult to replicate on the digital spectrum. To investigate this topic, Marshall and Bly [2005] conducted an in-depth observational study into the print and digital navigation methods of magazine users. After a thorough inspection of each participant's reading sessions, as well as a series of interviews and talk-throughs of reading habits, the authors confirmed that the general patterns of within-document navigation were roughly the same in the ePeriodical and paper versions of the magazine. The most intriguing observation made within the study is what the authors refer to as *lightweight navigation*:

> "navigation that occurs either when people reach a particular page or when they move within an article in a way that is so unselfconscious that they aren't apt to remember it later."
>
> — Marshall and Bly [2005]

This definition of the term *lightweight navigation* was defined in the context of linear reading: specifically, the unselfconscious, seamless movements that users make out of the linear stream of text and then back again. If an action is lightweight, then, the reader is seldom aware they are performing it. It is a useful way to describe the affordances that paper offers over digital.

Some examples of lightweight actions, as observed during the study are:

- Narrowing or broadening focus by manipulating the physical magazine;

- Letting one's eyes stray to a page element out of the textual flow;

- Looking ahead in the text to preview or anticipate;

- Looking back to re-read for context.

These properties, which are common activities on paper, are rarely seen in digital document navigation. For example, one of the major lightweight activities Marshall et al. observed was the act of page turning—described as a complex combination of lightweight navigational activities, a seamless interaction that, sadly, is absent from even the most sophisticated of digital page-turning simulations (such as British Library [1997]; Chu et al. [2003]).

These lightweight properties, therefore, are examples that are specific to the interactions with *physical* documents. Marshall and Bly speculate, however, that this concept of lightweight interaction can also be applied to digital technology, but do not give any concrete evidence to support it. There are many aspects of computerized technology that far exceed the capabilities of paper (i.e., searching, zooming, etc.), and by paying closer attention to the possibility of lightweight interaction, digital document software can not only incorporate the physical affordances of paper but also improve upon them by surpassing the limitations of paper.

The term lightweight is used frequently throughout this book to describe a task or action that can be performed without a significant amount of cognitive attention. In addition to this, we will also be referring to its corollary: heavyweight—which can be used to describe a task or action that takes a lot of conscious effort to perform.

3.2.1   PAPER VERSUS DIGITAL

There are many properties of paper that can be considered lightweight. There are also a large number of physical characteristics that make paper documents so popular. For example, paper is cheap and familiar compared to electronic equipment, it can be written on easily, and can also contain useful meta-data that are not implicitly available on digital documents (e.g., the *feel* or *heft* of the book).

In comparison, there are also several aspects of digital documents that exceed the limitations of paper. For example, digital documents are quick and easy to edit, copy, and search. They benefit from spell checkers, translators, and other computationally complex activities, and can be magnified to reveal more detail. It is also possible to store many thousands of digital documents easily and relatively cheaply on light and portable storage devices.

In short, there are benefits and drawbacks to both paper and digital texts. It is our intention, therefore, to combine some of the lightweight properties of paper with digital enhancements to improve the overall usability of electronic documents and hopefully identify what can be considered *digitally lightweight*.

3.3   COGNITION AND THE USER

Before embarking on an investigation into lightweight techniques, we describe the cognitive demands of users while they are engaged in demanding tasks such as active reading. This section describes several useful concepts that help describe the theoretical underpinnings of the lightweight interaction model.

3.3.1   READY-TO-HAND AND PRESENT-AT-HAND

The German philosopher Martin Heidegger [1962] originally coined two terms to explain the instinctive nature and attitudes toward things in the world. His ideas have greatly influenced the field of cognitive psychology and are also extremely relevant to the broad area of human-computer interaction [Winograd and Flores, 1985].

Ready-to-hand (*zuhanden*): describes a scenario where users are engaged with the world in a normal and involved way. Specifically, users are performing tasks without thinking about the mechanics or tools being used to facilitate them. For example, when using a mouse to manipulate menus on a computer, the user in this case is not thinking about the tool itself (i.e., the mouse), only the objects they are directing with it.

Present-at-hand (*vorhanden*): describes a situation where users are no longer thinking about the task at hand, but rather the tools that are facilitating the task. Users in this scenario are conscious of the physical object itself, for example, picking up a fork and thinking about its design as opposed to thinking about what they are eating. This state is extremely undesirable in HCI as it pulls the user's attention away from their primary task. Ideally, we would want users to be thinking about their primary task, *not* the tools that assist it.

When applied to the ideas proposed in this book, it would be beneficial for users to be thinking about their primary task (ready-to-hand), i.e., the active reading task, as opposed to thinking about the tools they use to do so (present-at-hand), i.e., the writing implements. In fact, we believe that a truly intuitive tool should only be present-at-hand when it is in a broken state and users are therefore thinking about how to fix it; at all other times it should be *invisible*.

3.3.2   INVISIBLE COMPUTERS

Another useful way of describing the ready-to-hand state is with *invisible computers* [Norman, 1998]. In his book *The Design of Everyday Things*, Norman [1988] suggests that computers should be made invisible in order to lend more time and attention to the task at hand:

> "When I use a direct manipulation system—whether for text editing, drawing pictures, or creating and playing games—I do think of myself not as using a computer but as doing the particular task. The computer is, in effect, invisible. The point cannot be overstressed: make the computer system invisible." — Norman [1988]

The idea of invisible computers is similar to those laid down by Marshall et al. and Heidegger: essentially, that the tools employed to complete a task should be so intuitive that they are, in effect, *hidden* from the user:

> "You don't notice the computer because you think of yourself doing the task, not as using the computer." — Norman [1988]

This concept has also been touched upon by Weiser [1993] who is considered by many as the founder of ubiquitous computing. Weiser thought that computers should 'get out of the way' or, essentially, that we should make technology disappear. Although this idea was originally defined for ubicomp, it also applies to the broader sense of human-computer interaction and ties in well with the other views described above.

In summary, therefore, computer systems should be designed to be as easy to use as possible, essentially rendering the tools themselves as *invisible*. If the technology is too complicated it can disrupt the user's primary task of reading and understanding the text—an undesirable situation that can lead to the loss of *flow* with the active reading task.

3.3.3   FLOW

Hungarian psychologist Mihaly Csikszentmihalyi first outlined the theory of *flow*, which suggests that people are most happy when they are in a state of complete concentration or absorption in a task. This level of attention is theorized as the point at which users reach the optimal state of *intrinsic motivation*, to the point at which they are so absorbed in the task at hand that all other considerations are forgotten. In his influential book *Flow: The Psychology of Optimal Experience*, Csikszentmihalyi [1990] defines the term as:

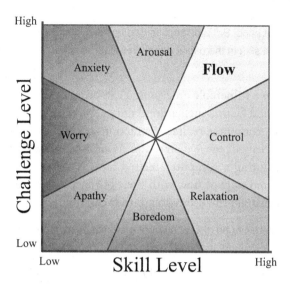

Figure 3.1: Csikszentmihalyi's [1997] mental state graph showing challenge versus skill level.

"The state in which people are so involved in an activity that nothing else seems to matter; the experience itself is so enjoyable that people will do it even at great cost, for the sheer sake of doing it."   — Csikszentmihalyi [1990]

This state of *flow*, also known colloquially as being 'in the zone,' 'on the ball,' or 'in the groove' is well illustrated in terms of challenge and skill level by the famous graph [Csikszentmihalyi, 1997] shown in Figure 3.1. From this illustration we can clearly see that in order to achieve the desired state of flow, there must be a balance between skill and challenge levels; that is, the skill level of the user and the challenge level of the task must both be high. If a task is too easy, or the skill level of the individual is too small, then the state of flow cannot be achieved.

When applied to the active reading process, it is beneficial for a system to encourage a state of flow with the primary task by making the tools themselves invisible, avoiding the undesirable present-at-hand state. For example, a user may be in the state of flow writing notes on a document; in this state they are not thinking about the tool they are using to make the notes (i.e., the pen). If, however, the pen runs out of ink during the process, their attention then shifts from the active reading task to the secondary task of repairing or replacing the pen, and the state of flow is consequently lost.

3.3.4   DISTRACTION

Pace [2004] discusses the possibility of distraction and how, in some cases, attention may be drawn involuntarily to stimuli outside the attentive focus [Eysenck and Keane, 2005].

> "Web users tend to ignore minor distractions during a flow experience because their attention is focused on the task at hand. But a distraction that has sufficient intensity, frequency or importance to cause a shift in the user's attention will terminate a flow experience."
>
> — Pace [2004]

As Pace notes, attention is a vulnerable process that can be easily diverted via a host of distractions. For example, environmental factors such as loud noises, physiological distractions such as hunger or fatigue, and, of course, computer-related distractions such as bugs, software error messages, or un-responsive programs, can all cause distraction. Poor user interface design can also contribute to the loss of attention during a computer-related task. Assuming, therefore, that the user has already achieved the desired state of flow with their primary active reading task, poorly designed tools may consequently distract the user enough to break them out of their task flow experience.

> "A poorly designed interface can disrupt a flow experience by demanding an excessive amount of attention."
>
> — Pace [2004]

This point is also highlighted by Marshall [1997] in an earlier paper on digital annotation.

> "switching midstream … is distracting. How much attention is … [a user] … expending to switch from 'annotate in the margin mode' … Will he still be engaged with the text after he has interacted with it?"
>
> — Marshall [1997]

Hence, reducing the level of attention required to use the tools required for active reading will consequently reduce distraction and therefore lessen the possibility of losing a flow state. This property can serve as an alternative definition or understanding of the term lightweight. Thus, making the tools used for active reading more lightweight will decrease the likelihood of losing a state of flow with the primary task.

The concept of flow, as it stands, is not a core topic of research in this book. However, it is relevant to demonstrate how the use of lightweight design can improve the usability of active reading systems. That is, the lightweight tools we create in this book do not necessarily aid in the creation of a flow state, but are intended to decrease the possibility of distracting the user away from an already achieved flow experience.

3.3.5   AFFORDANCE

There has been a significant amount of research into the concept of *affordance*, a term the Oxford English Dictionary describes as:

aff-or-dance (*noun*) A characteristic of an object, esp. relating to its potential utility, which can be inferred from visual or other perceptual signals; (more widely) a quality or utility which is readily apparent or available.

Although the term 'affordance' was first used by ecological psychologist J. J. Gibson [1977; 1979], in the context of human-computer interaction it was first used by Norman [1988] in his book

The Psychology of Everyday Things. What Norman is actually referring to is *perceived affordance*: specifically, whether or not the user perceives that some action is possible. Culturally, then, we are taught to expect certain things. For example, it is widely recognized that knobs are for turning, buttons are for pushing, and slots are for putting things into. As Norman commented:

> "An affordance is not a property, it is a relationship that holds between the organism that is acting on the object. The same object may have different affordances for different individuals."
>
> — Norman [1998]

An adult, for example, will usually look at everyday objects such as pens or keys in relation to the tasks they were designed to achieve, whereas a child will almost certainly regard them as tasty treats or playthings. The idea behind these affordances, then, is that if understood correctly, the user will know instinctively how to perform the appropriate actions, and possibly even do so without consciously thinking.

In contrast, if apparent affordances have no actual function, we have *false affordance*, a problem first noted by Gaver [1991], where people mistakenly try to use something in a way that is not in fact possible. For example, a door with a handle that actually needs to be pushed exhibits false affordance, as its presence indicates to the user that the handle should be used to pull the door.

Sellen and Harper [1997] have investigated how the properties of paper support document-related tasks. Although they agree paper offers many useful affordances, they stress that the digital equivalents do not need to mimic the properties of paper. Instead, they suggest that designers take into account these affordances and attempt to provide them in other ways. Tashman and Edwards [2011b] also stress a similar point:

> "Purely mimicking the affordances of paper in a computer-based system may not address all of the opportunities that digital technology can potentially provide."
>
> — Tashman and Edwards [2011b]

Clearly, therefore, slavishly replicating every physical interaction in the design of digital document tools is not the optimal way of enhancing them. However, by incorporating some of the more appropriate lightweight physical aspects into digital document design, we can not only reproduce some of the benefits of paper, but also surpass them by incorporating purely electronic techniques.

3.3.6   METAPHORS

One concept that follows on from the notion of affordance is the visual *metaphor*.

met-a-phor (*noun*) A figure of speech in which a word or phrase is applied to an object or action to which it is not literally applicable; a thing regarded as representative or symbolic of something else, especially something abstract.

In the context of HCI, the term *metaphor* can be used to describe the visual relationship users have between a computer interface and real-world objects. For example, the common raised button seen in many modern graphical user interfaces, being slightly three-dimensional in appearance, resembles a physical button, and therefore implicitly suggests it should be pushed. This type of metaphorical representation of a real-world object takes advantage of users' intrinsic knowledge of the world and applies a new set of affordances to an electronic depiction of a physical interaction.

When designing a new metaphor, it is important to carefully consider how best to represent an interaction that is currently prominent in the physical plane. Some experts believe that if a digital interaction does not fully comply to the manner consistent with the looks and associations of the physical counterpart, then it will confuse users to the point at which their performance will suffer. Heim [2007], for example, states:

> "A metaphor's function must be consistent with real-world expectations ... metaphors should be employed to facilitate learning; they should not contradict the user's previous knowledge."
>
> — Heim [2007]

Although this seems reasonable, there are other researchers who argue that by following this rationale, in some cases, designers can fall into the trap of attempting to create a virtual metaphor of a physical object that is in itself badly designed. Sharp et al. [2011] give the example of an old type of virtual calculator which was, at the time, designed to look and behave like a real-world calculator—a device that was poorly designed even in its physical form.

Before transferring a metaphor from the physical world to the digital domain, then, it is essential to the overall usability of the final interface that any real-world metaphor is carefully chosen. In short, metaphors should not be forced [Heim, 2007]. Rather, only the more intuitive and familiar real-world metaphors should be translated to the digital level.

3.4   SUMMARY

In this chapter we have described a set of concepts and literature that are central to the work described in this book. Our investigations into both paper-based and on-screen reading have given a clearer picture of the shortcomings of digital reading and the psychology behind this outcome.

It is clear from the majority of the literature [Dillon, 1992; Muter et al., 1982; O'Hara and Sellen, 1997; Wästlund et al., 2008] that paper is a faster and more popular medium than computer screens for attentive reading of a document. The reasoning behind this preference is linked to the affordances offered by physical documents and tools. The lightweight properties of paper enable often subconscious actions that divert very little cognitive attention from the primary active reading task.

Paper boasts many intuitive and tangible assets that enable smooth and unperturbed interactions from its users. One way to mimic parts of these interactions is by a transfer of metaphors from the physical plane—a concept we follow closely throughout the design decisions within this book.

One common way researchers in the area have made use of metaphors is by mimicking the interactions with physical books. When a metaphor is created, it provides its function with a certain set of affordances. The book metaphor, then, supplies particular affordances for functions such as page turning, placeholding, annotation, and so on. The majority of the literature seen in the area of digital document design focuses strongly on the physical book metaphor by using it in some way when creating and improving digital reading interfaces. For instance, there has been a significant body of work that focuses on augmented reading hardware by transferring eDocuments to portable book-shaped reading devices and enhancing them with paper-like tangibility [Hinckley et al., 2009; Marshall et al., 1999; Tashman and Edwards, 2011b].

Other researchers have opted for the solely software route by closely mimicking the visual interaction styles of paper in realistic electronic books [British Library, 1997; Card et al., 2004; Chu et al., 2003]. Other common areas of investigation are concerned with the amalgamation of physical documents with digital enhancements [Liao et al., 2008; Wellner, 1991], which typically involves keeping the physical tangibility of the paper book while improving it with electronic features.

The digital tools we implement to aid in the digital active reading process will often be designed around lightweight physical attributes by transferring metaphors from paper. In some situations, we will also be utilizing solely electronic properties to create the same digitally lightweight properties. In both cases, however, the tools we design should strive to be lightweight and ready-to-hand to ensure the maximum amount of cognitive attention can be paid to the primary task as opposed to the tools themselves. This will then reduce the possibility that the tools will distract the user out of a flow state with the primary active reading task. With this in mind, the main motivations for this book are to prove by example that lightweight interaction is possible in digital documents in order to produce a list of attributes that can be considered digitally lightweight to aid in future designs of active reading software.

CHAPTER 4

Lightweight Interactions

4.1 INTRODUCTION

In this chapter we describe four areas of digital reading to which we apply lightweight interaction principles. These four areas have been chosen specifically to investigate both actions that are currently easy to perform on paper but have proven themselves cumbersome digitally, and actions that are currently difficult to perform both digitally and physically. This allows us to migrate some of the more lightweight properties from the physical to the digital domain, as well as taking advantage of digital-only techniques. We start with the common activity of placeholding, a lightweight action on paper, but one which has been badly translated to the digital plane. Moving on from this, we look at annotation, first analyzing how it is performed on paper, which then allows us to tailor a more suitable digital solution. Combining these first two sections, we then take a look at how to amalgamate both placeholding and annotation into a single tool, mimicking the use of paper. Finally, we look at indexing—a topic that can be considered heavyweight both physically and digitally. Our final example demonstrates an indexing method that combines properties from both mediums to create an digitally lightweight solution. From each of these four focus areas, we draw out lightweight interaction guidelines that we suggest will be important for the design of future digital reading devices.

4.2 PLACEHOLDERS

Placeholders in physical documents are a long-established method of locating information, providing crucial support for readers in remembering important places in the text. Placeholders can take many different forms. Scrap paper, dog-eared corners, bookmarks, or even fingers that are used as location aids [Dillon, 1992] require minimal effort, making them a perfect example of lightweight navigation. Unfortunately, however, the equivalent tools on digital documents are  far less intuitive, and are consequently a more time consuming and cumbersome affair. In fact, much of the literature on this topic confirms that digital placeholders in their current form are extremely poorly used despite recommendations from experts that they should be simple to achieve [Wilson and Landoni, 2003].

Placeholders, then, are a perfect example of an area which is lightweight on paper yet heavyweight electronically. In this section we investigate both paper and digital placeholding, and discuss a potential design for lightweight digital placeholders.

4.2.1   BACKGROUND

Reading is rarely entirely linear. There are many occasions, even when reading more linear texts, such as novels, when the reader may decide to revisit a previous section to clarify or refresh their perception of the text, or perhaps peek ahead for a sneak preview. Several studies have touched on the importance of document revisitation. Marshall and Bly [2005], for example, documented magazine readers' usage of placeholders for re-reading, refreshing, or double checking, whereas O'Hara [1996] states the importance of re-reading in learning situations. There has also been research into the frequency of revisitations on digitized media. Greenberg and Witten [1993] studied the reuse of Unix command lines, and found that three quarters of commands actually exist in the history list; that is, that three out of four are in fact revisitations as opposed to new commands. It is clear from the literature, then, that the revisitation of pages within documents is a key reading activity, and one that should be carefully considered when making the transition from paper to digital reading.

Placeholder Types

Placeholders are used in many different forms, ranging from ribbons or bookmarks in physical books to page markers or headings in digital documents. Each of these different types of placeholders can be considered to be either *temporary* or *permanent*. For example, a bookmark or a finger [Dillon, 1992; O'Hara and Sellen, 1997] can be used to temporarily mark a place, but are then typically removed and placed elsewhere (i.e., when reading a novel, you may slip in a bookmark when you go and get a snack, then remove it again when you resume reading). A document is likely to have only one temporary placeholder within it, which is usually placed solely to remember a particular place within the text. Sticky notes are an example of more permanent placeholders that can be used to mark pages that are often looked for (i.e., a chapter in a textbook that contains an important piece of information). A document will often contain multiple permanent placeholders which are designed for long-term revisitation of commonly used sections. There are also techniques that could be considered to be *semi*-permanent placeholders. For example, folding down the corner of a page, or 'dog-earing' [Rosner et al., 2008], as it is often referred, is a method of placeholding that requires no external materials. It does, however, cause slight damage to the book itself, making it an undesirable long-term placeholder.

Physical Placeholders

There are many ways to hold a particular page within a paper document. Some examples of placeholders in physical documents can be seen in Figure 4.1. Placeholders are extremely common in physical documents, and are frequently employed without a significant amount of conscious

(a) 'Dog-eared' corner   (b) Arrow markers   (c) Book with built in ribbon marker   (d) See-through sticky note tab markers

Figure 4.1: Examples of physical placeholders.

effort from the user. As well as marking a place within a text, however, physical placeholders can also provide other implicit information to the user. For example, placing a sticky note half way down a particular page could indicate that the first half of the page has already been read. As Heim [2007] states:

> "Paper documents afford the use of place holders and allow us to make determinations of text length and location within the text." — Heim [2007]

Digital Placeholders

Digital placeholders are essentially links to specific points within text, and typically take the form of a list. The most common forms of digital placeholders are: web-bookmarking (Figure 4.2(a)), digital document bookmarks (Figure 4.2(b) and 4.2(c)), and electronic reading device bookmarks (Figure 4.2(d)).

More commonly known as 'favorites,' web bookmarks generally take the form of a menu; that is, they usually exist within a drop down menu structure and are ordered according to the date in which they were added (see Figure 4.2(a) for an example). Web bookmarks are not used to place marks within documents, but rather to keep an overall record of entire documents. Research into the observed usage of web page bookmarks has been a popular topic since early on in their development. It has been well documented that web bookmarking is more commonly used as a long-term archival aid as opposed to a method of relocating well-known material. Abrams et al. [1998], for example, discovered that frequency of use was not a factor in determining whether or not a page was bookmarked, with users commonly choosing to memorize URLs or use search engines to locate commonly visited sites.

The infrequent use of web bookmarks for revisitation was also investigated by Tauscher and Greenberg [1997] who focus on *how* people revisit web pages, and define the 'recurrence rate' of a page as the probability that a visited page is a repeat of a previous page visit (expressed as a percentage). With a revisitation result of 58% from their user study, they concluded that although the web is a 'recurrent system,' the use of bookmarks as a revisitation tool was very limited. Cock-

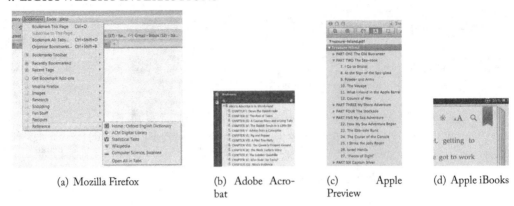

(a) Mozilla Firefox (b) Adobe Acrobat (c) Apple Preview (d) Apple iBooks

Figure 4.2: Examples of digital placeholders.

burn and McKenzie [2001] concur with these findings after a study into the Netscape history and bookmark files of a set of users. They discovered that 81% of page visits were revisitations, and that most people have large web bookmark lists. They suggested, however, that very few users make constant use of the bookmarks they have, and, furthermore, that the lists tend to grow over time but are rarely maintained, leading to sometimes overwhelmingly large and unmanageable bookmark collections. Realizing this problem, some researchers have investigated means to provide suitable organization for web favorites (e.g., Keller et al. [1997]; Tabard et al. [2007]; Weinreich et al. [2006]), but have generally reaffirmed the conclusion that web bookmarks are poorly used and do not sufficiently support web page revisitation.

The key result of over a decade of research in this area, therefore, is that the majority of web bookmarks are used for archival purposes (i.e., when users want a permanent record of a particular page) as opposed to a general form of revisitation.

A web page can be considered as a non-paginated document, or a set of linked documents. In either case, however, 'bookmarking' a web page will result in a placeholder to the document *as a whole* as opposed to a specific portion. Clearly, then, the concept of web bookmarking does not provide the same functionality as classic placeholders do in physical books. In contrast to web favorites, paginated document readers allow bookmarks to be made on specific portions of a document, typically single pages, facilitating, in effect, sub-document bookmarking of the type found in physical books.

Surprisingly, given its popularity on the physical plane, within-document bookmarking on paginated digital texts has been little studied. Marshall and Bly [2005] touched upon this topic briefly while making a comparison between user behaviors on physical and digital texts. The results from this portion of the study indicated that users rate digital bookmarking tools harshly compared to their physical equivalents, and also make less use of them. Other studies of electronic document usage have also touched upon the lack of bookmarks within digital texts, but often with less direct evidence [Woodward et al., 1998].

Placeholders within digital document readers usually take the form of an ordered list; that is, they usually exist in a tree structure to one side of the interface, and are ordered by page number (see Figure 4.2(b) for an example). The way in which these structured lists behave is also drastically different to the way placeholders are used on paper, resulting in the loss of many intuitive functions. For example, on paper it is easy to see where a bookmark is in relation to the current page by simply observing which bookmarks stick out of pages before and after the current position. Some digital document readers provide a function for this (e.g., Apple's Preview highlights the appropriate bookmark when a page is changed), whereas others (e.g., Adobe's Acrobat) only highlight the current bookmark when a user explicitly clicks in the bookmark list. Other useful information that has not migrated from paper to digital bookmarking is the ability to see the spread of where bookmarks exist within the document. For example, on paper it would be easy to see if a large document had all its bookmarks concentrated in the first 20 pages, whereas the majority of digital readers bookmark lists do not show this information.

Several research groups have recognized that current electronic bookmarking tools bear no resemblance to their physical counterparts, and have attempted to make digital bookmarks more paper-like in order to bridge the gap and increase user uptake of the tools available (e.g., Card et al. [2004]; Liesaputra et al. [2009a]).

As well as desktop document readers, it is also important to consider the bookmark functions included within dedicated reading devices such as eReaders. The majority of eReader devices indicate bookmarked pages by displaying a small 'dog-ear' or ribbon in a corner of the reading area (Figure 4.2(d)). Even reading applications designed for portable computing devices (e.g., iPhones or iPads) use this method for distinguishing between bookmarked pages. The major drawback of this method, however, is that you must navigate to a page to know that it is bookmarked—there is usually no other way to tell where bookmarks exist while actually reading a document. In order to view all bookmarks within a document on one of these devices, the user usually has to navigate away from the document itself, and then find the bookmarks list separately. These bookmark lists are almost identical to those found on traditional desktop document readers, and therefore give little overview of where each bookmark is located in relation to others in the document. These types of placeholders can be considered permanent, as the reader must explicitly instruct the device to remove them. In addition to these dedicated bookmark functions, many eReader devices also record the last place the reader was at before exiting, a function that can be characterized as a temporary placeholder.

Current Placeholder Use

How often people use bookmarks is often dependent on what type of document they are using. Previous work has not provided a clear picture of the distribution of placeholder use between

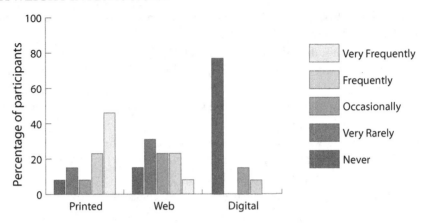

Figure 4.3: The frequency of placeholder use on printed, web, and digital documents.

digital and physical documents, however. To determine how placeholders are used in everyday situations, we performed a small user study to compare between printed, web, and digital media.

On average the results for placeholder use on printed documents take the form shown in Figure 4.3, with over two thirds of people using placeholders either frequently (about half the time) or very frequently (almost all documents). However, several users noted that their placeholder behavior differed significantly between novels and reference books. Novels, for example, typically favor a single temporary placeholder (i.e., a bookmark which is removed and replaced in a different spot every time the book is read), whereas reference books tend to include multiple more long-term markers (i.e., sticky tabs to mark useful sections). These differences in placeholder use often dictate how often they are used. For example, one user stated, "I never use bookmarks in novels, and hardly ever in reference books, but I use them in my bible all the time," while another said "I usually remember the page number in novels, but I do use them in text books quite a lot."

As Figure 4.3 shows, the differences between placeholder usage for printed and digital documents are substantial. The study found that 46% of people make very frequent (i.e., almost all documents) use of printed placeholders. In contrast, not a single person in this study made use of digital placeholders this frequently. In fact, 77% said that they had never used a placeholder in a digital document. For web-based placeholders (i.e., bookmarks), the results were mixed, and do not indicate a general preference either way.

This result shows that, of the three placeholder methods tested, paper is the most frequently used, with web bookmarking used slightly less frequently, and digital placeholding trailing—over three quarters of the people in our study had never used digital placeholders.

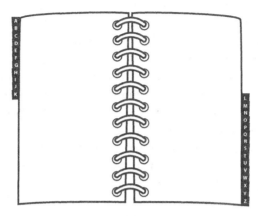

Figure 4.4: Example of telephone directory tabs. When the book is closed, there is of course only a single line of tabs, rather than the two visible here at the far left and far right edges of the pages.

4.2.2 LIGHTWEIGHT PLACEHOLDERS

As we have seen, placeholding on physical documents can be considered very lightweight—adding and removing bookmarks to paper documents can be so subconscious that users are unlikely to think about how they are doing it. In contrast, however, current digital placeholders are significantly less intuitive, and are consequently rated unfavorably against their physical equivalents. Although some systems (e.g., eReaders) make use of 'dog-eared' visualizations to signify bookmarked pages, the classical bookmark 'list' structure found in the majority of digital document readers is vastly different from paper, making lightweight actions difficult.

To bridge the gap between the physical and digital forms of placeholding, we implemented a system that constructs digital bookmark 'tabs' that mimic the way bookmarks are presented in physical books [Buchanan and Pearson, 2008]. These tabs are designed to give a visual representation of placeholders within a document. This feature ensures that the placeholders are *always* visible, as opposed to only being seen while on a bookmarked page.

The new lightweight placeholder tabs in our system are positioned in the virtual space located on either the right or left hand side of document. The design of this representation has been modeled in the style of a telephone directory; that is, bookmarks that occur before the current page appear on the left of the document, whereas bookmarks on the current or later pages appear on the right (see Figure 4.4). When the current page is changed, these tabs then 'flip' from one side to the other depending upon where they exist in relation to the open page. To make the relocation process easier for the user, the tabs are also ordered by page number, so the later the page, the further down the display the tab appears. Thus, a bookmark on page 1 will always appear at the top left corner of the display, whereas a bookmark on the last page will be seen on the bottom right. Due to the placement of these tabs (i.e., outside the document), they are always visible independent of the currently open page. This ensures that all bookmarks can be seen at all times, as opposed to the 'dog ear' or ribbon style interfaces seen in devices such as eReaders or tablet reading applications.

In addition to the colorful tabs, we also wanted to allow text to be added to bookmarks. However, we felt that it would be clumsy to allow text to be added to the bookmarks themselves, as word-wrapping and space issues would cause the display to look cluttered. Instead, to give an overview of the attributes associated with a particular bookmark, we added mouse-over pop-ups that display the title, description, page number, and appropriate border color of each placeholder. These pop-ups appear when the mouse is hovered over a tab, and provide the user with quick and easy access to each placeholder's information.

Since placeholders are traditionally bound by *pages* and not by paragraphs or sentences, we chose *single page display* pagination for the interface. This type of page display ensures that whole pages will always be visible when a bookmark is clicked. Continuous displays were not a suitable option for this system as it would be difficult and potentially confusing to users to illustrate where bookmarks that exist on previous and future pages are placed in relation to the user's current position.

Figure 4.5 shows our prototype interface, and illustrates the colorful tabs designed to mimic physical bookmarks. The physical size of each of these bookmark tabs is dependent upon how many are placed—the height of each tab is calculated by dividing the height of the document-viewing area by the number of bookmarks. Creating a new bookmark (and, similarly, deleting an existing bookmark) will resize and reorder every tab on the screen.

The aim of this implementation was to allow users to quickly and easily relocate and return to information in a document. This interaction was achieved by using a visual representation that mimics methods used in the physical domain (specifically utilizing the 'virtual' space surrounding the document itself). Each bookmark in the system can be distinguished by its color as well as its position in the display, and clicking on a tab will take the user directly to the bookmarked page.

To investigate the usability of our design, a short comparative user evaluation was carried out. A full discussion of this study can be found in our accompanying paper [Buchanan and Pearson, 2008]. Participants in the study used three systems—our new lightweight interface, a traditional un-ordered menu, and a standard chapter-headed bookmark list. For each of these, participants performed several reading and placeholder tasks. Our new system was the preferred method of placeholding, with the ordered list rated second and the un-ordered menu least preferred.

4.2.3   LIGHTWEIGHT PROPERTIES

After implementing and evaluating our visual bookmark system, several lightweight properties became apparent. Firstly, it was clear from user study results that the new visual tabs were the preferred way of displaying placeholders digitally. One key reason for this popularity, as described

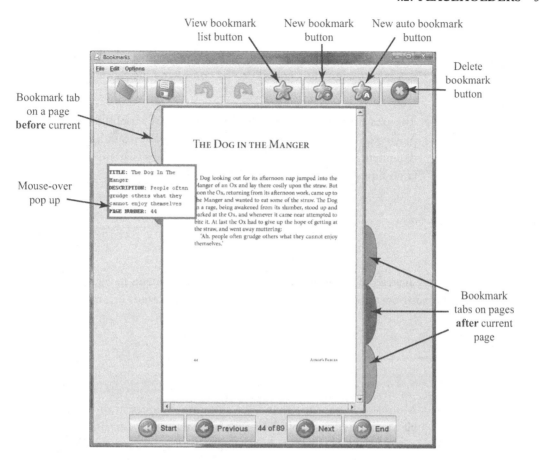

Figure 4.5: Our visual tabbed design.

by several participants, is the visual aspect of the design. That is, the shape, position, and color of the bookmark tabs. Being placed outside the document area, the tabs are *always* visible, ensuring they can be seen regardless of the currently open page. Unlike many placeholder tools that display their bookmarks in drop down lists (e.g., web browsers) or those that indicate bookmarked pages by icons on the pages themselves (e.g., eReader devices), the tabs in our design are static and are visible at all times. Lists are not always the best way of displaying information digitally—particularly if they are hidden within menus. The un-ordered menu system performed poorly in the study when compared to the ordered list system, suggesting that

- Hiding contextual information such as bookmarks within menus is a poor design choice, and can be considered 'heavyweight' if the function is frequently accessed;

- The area surrounding the document is potentially useful for displaying information. In this case, the static area surrounding the document was used to display the bookmark tabs that are visible at all times independently of the currently open page.

In addition to this, instead of locating information via clicks or menu navigation, our visual tab design utilizes mouse-over pop-ups to automatically display important information. So:

- Mouse-over pop-ups that allow important information to be viewed easily by simply hovering the cursor over certain areas of the screen can provide lightweight information at a glance.

Another area of digital document placeholding that can be considered heavyweight if performed incorrectly is the ability to see where bookmarks exist in relation to each other, as well as in relation to the currently open page—something that is achieved painlessly on paper. The tabbed nature of the bookmarks in our new lightweight system ensures the user can see exactly how many there are within a document, as well as providing an easy method of navigation. The system's bookmarks have been specifically designed in telephone directory style to clearly show their location in relation to each other (i.e., a bookmark at the top is further toward the beginning of the document than one at the bottom), as well as their relation to the current page (i.e., bookmarks on the left occur on pages before the current page and ones on the right occur after the current page). Therefore:

> • A visual approach, in this case using the *position* of the tabs to indicate where in the document they are positioned, is a good way of illustrating important information. This also gives a neat overview of where each bookmark exists in relation to each other, as well as in relation to the currently open page.

Using color was also highlighted as a useful way of distinguishing between items in a list (for example, using red to indicate important pages). Therefore:

> • The use of color may be a lightweight property if used effectively.

In summary, our evaluation of an example lightweight visual tab bookmark design has identified several potentially lightweight properties that will be useful for future lightweight digital reading designs. Some of these are investigated in greater depth in later sections, helping to refine their relevance to the active reading process.

4.3   ANNOTATIONS

Annotation and note-taking are very common active reading activities. Previous investigations into annotation have confirmed that when working on documents, nearly half of user time is spent annotating or note-taking [Adler et al., 1998]. Research into the use of digital annotations, however, has consistently reported their low popularity and lack of use [O'Hara and Sellen, 1997; Sellen and Harper, 2003]. It is clear from the literature, then, the value of mark-up is high, yet the uptake on digital media is low—making it an ideal area for investigation into lightweight design.

Our investigation into digital placeholders found that the space surrounding a document was a useful area to display information. This lightweight property could also apply to annotations—an area that is currently described as being unintuitive digitally [Marshall and Bly, 2005; O'Hara and Sellen, 1997; Sellen and Harper, 2003]. With this in mind, we now turn to focus on the role of marginal space in improving the support for active reading in digital documents.

4.3.1 BACKGROUND

The topic of annotation has been studied in great depth by a number of researchers over the last few decades. One such research program [O'Hara et al., 1998] found that the majority of annotations made (on photocopied documents) were placed in the margin area, and confirmed that in most cases users wrote short notes or brief, incomplete phrases, rather than large complete sentences. The authors observed from this that the meaning of these annotations was highly dependent upon the textual context to which they relate, and commented that the annotations were not independently interpretable; rather, they are distinguishable only with the original text to which they are linked. This result suggests that the positioning of annotations is an important factor in the active reading process, as poorly positioned notes may be hard to link back to the original content to which they relate.

Marshall [1998] also conducted an investigation into work-related annotation by studying the marks made on textbooks in a university bookstore. The particular store studied provided a 'buy back' scheme, which allowed students to sell their previously used books, along with any annotations, back to the store after use. Marshall uses the observations from this study to categorize several ways in which users associate annotations with printed document elements. She states that users making marginal notes generally connect them to the source text in one of three ways: using arrows; using a bracket, brace, or some other mark; or, sometimes even relying on proximity alone to connect their own marginal (or interline) jottings with the text. Any attempt to recreate the physical annotation process digitally must therefore ensure a complete set of tools is incorporated to allow all the types of anchoring mentioned by Marshall and others.

Physical Annotations

Annotations on physical documents can take two general forms: the informal markings users make on a page while reading and professional scholarly annotations found in literary works [Marshall, 2009]. The latter here refers to critical edition books, such as the extract from *Cliffs Complete Annotated Macbeth* shown in Figure 4.6. These professionally annotated versions of popular literature are intended to aid readers in the comprehension of classic and scholarly material, and do so without altering the format of the original text. The example in Figure 4.6 shows to the lower left the original Shakespeare text and in the other areas the annotations put in by the publisher. The original text, in this case Act I, Scene I of *Macbeth* has not been altered; instead annotations have been included in the extended margins.

A more common type of annotations made on documents are informal markings made by the user while reading and making sense of the text. These markings, which are commonly referred to as notes, annotations, or scribbles, can include (but are not limited to): highlights, underlining, circling, doodling, and text. Figure 4.7 shows four examples of informal user markings that show

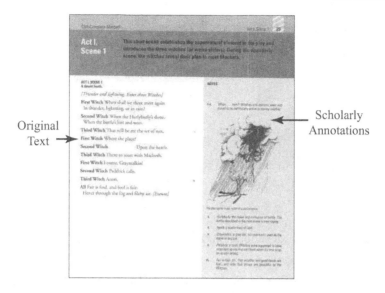

Original Text

Scholarly Annotations

Figure 4.6: An extract from *Cliffs Complete Annotated Macbeth.*

a diverse range of physical annotation possibilities. Figure 4.7(a), for example, shows a simple highlight; Figure 4.7(b) depicts the use of personalized symbols within the margin; Figure 4.7(c) uses a connector (in this case an arrow) to link the source material to an annotation; and Figure 4.7(d) shows an example of a key coding system that separates out different characters' speech dialogues.

One issue regarding the annotation of pre-existing literature that has been little investigated to date is *where* the marks are made. Ideally (for the reader) the notes would be made close to the text to which they relate—for example, writing a definition next to a word in a textbook would keep it in context. The problem in this instance, however, is that it is not always possible to make notes close to the text. Writing over the document itself may obscure the original text, whereas writing in the margins provides finite space and could prove difficult to make a connection between the annotation and the text.

Another potential problem with both of these solutions is that writing over the text or even in the margins damages the original document—an issue that has drawn mixed opinions from readers [Jackson, 2002]. A potential solution to this problem is to write the notes on a separate medium (e.g., spare paper, sticky notes, notebooks, etc.). Although this approach does give potentially unlimited space for writing notes, it now means that it can be difficult to reference specific locations within the original document, and an annotation could easily get separated from the text to which it relates. Another solution to the problem of damaging the original document is to buy specialist note-taking equipment. The note tabs shown in Figure 4.1(d), for example, are

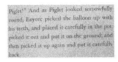

(a) Highlighting   (b) Margin marks   (c) Connections between   (d) Key system
                                                    source text and user an-
                                                    notations

Figure 4.7: Examples of physical annotation.

sticky semi-transparent notes that act as placeholders and allow users to make notes and highlights on a document without damaging the document itself.

Digital Annotations

Annotations within electronic documents are often considered unintuitive, with some researchers even describing them as "cumbersome" [O'Hara and Sellen, 1997]. One of the most popular digital reading applications on the market today is Adobe Acrobat Reader, which is free for download and is available on Windows, Mac, and Linux platforms. Unlike older versions, the current version of the software (Adobe Acrobat X or version 10.0, at the time of writing) also includes a small number of annotation features which were previously only available in the Professional edition. These features include text highlighting and sticky notes, which can be seen in Figure 4.8(a). The pay-to-use Adobe Acrobat Professional edition of the software includes additional annotation tools such as call outs, shapes, text underlining, and so on.

Apple's Preview application also allows simple annotations to be made to existing PDF documents in a similar style to Acrobat (see Figure 4.8(b)). The sticky note feature in this application forces notes to be made in the left-hand margin of the screen, and gives little flexibility to reorder and organize the notes within this area.

In its latest versions, Microsoft Word has also included a commenting feature which allows text to be highlighted and comments to be added. This feature, which is aimed at collaborative editing, again forcibly stores comments in one margin of the screen—see Figure 4.8(c).

Anatomy of Annotation

Researchers in the field of digital libraries have endeavored to understand the different styles of annotation. For example, Agosti et al. [2006] studied historic practices of annotation, and the development of a digital library infrastructure to capture marginalia and other marks on medieval

(a) Adobe Acrobat Reader X

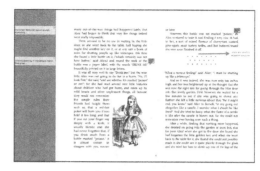

(b) Apple Preview version 5

(c) Microsoft Word 2007

Figure 4.8: Examples of digital annotation.

documents. By providing a consistent terminology for the different parts of digital annotation (e.g., Agosti et al. [2004]), it is possible to create a universal representation that facilitates the creation of usable annotations in digital documents. With this in mind, it seems sensible to first distinguish between the different parts of annotations in order to better understand how to create a complete digital solution. Marshall [2009] describes three separate elements of annotations:

Body: Any content added to the original document by the reader (e.g., a note or star written in the margin).

Anchor: The portion of the original text to which the annotation relates.

Marker: How the anchor should be rendered when displayed (i.e., the type and color of writing implement used).

To take an example, in Figure 4.7(c), the *body* is the handwritten text 'Ashdown Forest, Sussex. 100 Acre Wood,' its *anchor* is the source text 'middle of the forest,' and its *marker* is a black rectangle. Similarly, Figure 4.7(a), has an empty *body* (i.e., there is no additional content added by the user), its *anchor* is the text 'Eeyore picked the balloon up with his teeth,' and its *marker* is a yellow highlight.

Digital implementations offer several other useful annotation elements that would be tricky and time consuming to replicate on paper. For example: the *author* which records who created the annotation, and the *time stamp* which keeps a record of exactly when the annotation was made. While it is unlikely that many such complex and complete annotations will be seen on paper, it is useful to have a set of common terms that will facilitate the discussion and comparison of annotations independent of implementation or platform.

It is clear from the examples in Figure 4.7(b) that annotations are made up of several elements and can take many different forms. Therefore, providing just one tool to support such a feature, as many digital systems do, is not a complete solution. To create a complete toolset for a digital implementation, then, these different annotation elements must be studied in more detail, in order to provide the appropriate tools for the jobs at hand. We will therefore be using this anatomy of annotation as a grounding for the design of the toolset in an improved digital solution, as well as a base for evaluating if it is indeed the *minimal* complete set of tools.

Marginalia

One of the key concepts in annotation is the idea of marginal notes or *marginalia*:

mar-gi-na-li-a (*plural noun*) Notes, commentary, and similar material written or printed in the margin of a book or manuscript. Also (in extended use): notes, comments, etc., which are incidental or additional to the main topic.

There are many famous figures who are known for their marginalia (e.g., Samuel Taylor Coleridge—see the collection in Coleridge [2003]); in this case, of course, a reader's notes can significantly increase the overall value of an otherwise 'damaged' document. The act of writing notes in the margin of a printed document has been around probably for as long as there have been margins to write in, providing a useful space to make notes to aid memory and communication. Jackson [2002] has investigated the concept of marginalia in depth, from casual scribbles to lengthy arguments, by studying the use of thousands of annotated books from a time span of over three centuries. After referring to readers' annotations as "a familiar but unexplained phenomenon," Jackson then reflects on the cultural and historical value of marginalia and presents a detailed review of some of the more interesting and famous examples in history.

The use of margins to place notes is a common occurrence in the physical world, but there have been occasions when researchers have encountered complaints from study participants with regard to the lack of marginal space on digital documents. Marshall et al. [1999], for example, observed several user criticisms over the XLibris system's (see Section 2.3.5) lack of marginal space:

> "One reader complained that the margins, which were reduced when we scanned in the paper, were too small for marginalia. We have observed this complaint in other uses of XLibris as well.

This emphasizes the importance of large margins for encouraging annotation, but it also introduces a design trade-off. Assuming a fixed size display, and scanned or pre-formatted documents (e.g., Postscript or PDF), increasing margin size ultimately decreases readability."

— Marshall et al. [1999].

This evidence suggests that marginalia can form an important part of the active reading process on both physical and digital documents. To investigate this issue further, and to verify exactly where the most common and popular areas for annotation are located, we first conducted a comparison study on paper-based material. The results of this study were then used as a grounding for the design of a digital annotation system which we evaluate later in this section.

Current Annotation Use

There have been a variety of studies that have focused on how users annotate on printed documents. However, a topic that has thus far been overlooked is where these annotations are positioned. Superficially, this issue is straightforward: annotations will appear near to the material to which they relate—for example, a circle around a word within a paragraph and an arrow pointing to a definition somewhere in the margin. The problem faced with annotations on printed documents is that space is finite, and this can potentially force additional mark-ups to be made outside the desired area, or even on additional media. This scenario consequently presents the problem of referencing the separate annotation back to the original text. As we have discovered from the literature (e.g., O'Hara et al. [1998]), the concept of space has value within active reading systems, yet so far there has been little research on the topic of exactly where is the best place to position notes.

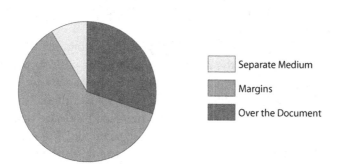

Figure 4.9: The distribution of users' annotation locations on paper.

On physical documents, there are three distinct locations where annotations can be placed:

1. Over the document itself;

2. In the margins of the document;

3. On a separate medium.

All of these locations suffer from potential problems, however. For example, annotating over the document itself obscures the original text, whereas writing on a separate medium makes it hard to reference related material within the document. Actual user behaviors are currently unclear as surprisingly little research in the area of annotation location has been undertaken.

To understand people's current use of paper-based annotation, therefore, we performed a small evaluation to investigate mark-up locations. This study compared users' annotation placements on two documents: one with large margins and one with no margins.

The results of this investigation indicated that the vast majority of people (90% of users in this study) thought that having more space around the outside of the document is useful when marking up. Figure 4.9 shows the distribution of users' annotation locations on paper illustrating that the margins are by far the preferred location, possibly because this location offers the strongest link with the subject of the annotation.

The documents used in the study were draft-like copies of hardback books; that is, they were simply ring-bound documents printed on standard office paper. When prompted about annotating their own purchased or borrowed books in the post-study interview, all participants admitted that they would never annotate the book itself for fear of damaging it. There was a mixed reaction to whether or not a separate medium is a resolution to the problem of annotation on documents with little or no margin. There were three positive points given: that they offer potentially unlimited space; they do not obscure the original document text; and, they do not damage the original document. However, participants also raised three issues associated with using a separate annotation medium: their tendency to get lost or detached from the original text; that separate notes mean little without the original text to refer to; and, that it is hard to reference a specific section in the original text on a separate medium.

Clearly, people enjoy the freedom of physically writing on the document, whether it is on top of the original text or in the margins, as annotating close to the section of literature to which you are referring keeps the notes in context. Participants were worried about damaging the original copy, but this is a problem that need not affect a digital solution. When designing a new digital annotation system, provisions can be made to ensure that the original document remains unaffected by saving the annotations in a separate file. This will overcome the problems associated with damaging the original text, as notes can be toggled on and off, and also allow multiple annotation files to be associated with a single copy of the document.

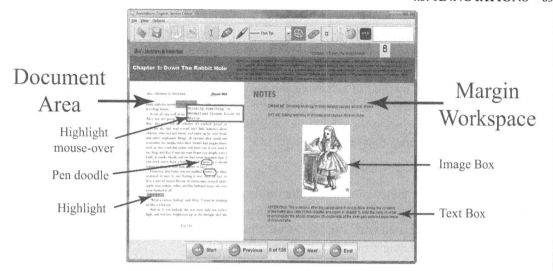

Figure 4.10: Lightweight digital annotation interface.

4.3.2 LIGHTWEIGHT ANNOTATIONS

In the physical world there is a lot of space surrounding documents, including not just the immediate document area, such as the margins, but the additional space around the paper such as walls and the desk area. Electronically, however, notes are normally limited to the document area itself. This space can be categorized into two distinct types:

Margins Document margins give each individual page additional space surrounding the document text to make notes. Therefore, each page's margin belongs to the page itself and turning to a new page gives a fresh margin. Notes in this form can be made on the document directly, or by sticking or inserting a separate medium (e.g., sticky notes).

Static Space Other types of additional space in which notes can be made about a document include static space which stays constant independent of the open page—for example, placing sticky notes on the desk or the wall close to the space where the user is working. This type of additional space ensures that the content of the annotation can always be seen, despite the currently open page.

To explore the potential for improving digital annotation, we implemented a digital reading system with expandable margins (see Figure 4.10). Unlike our earlier placeholders system, where the area outside the document was static, and remained constant despite the currently open page, our annotation design makes use of margins that are linked to specific pages, as in physical books. Therefore, each page has its own separate margin area, the content of which is only visible on the screen when that particular page is open.

As we discovered during our investigation into physical annotation, users are reluctant to annotate their own books, as they do not want to damage them. This preference is something that can easily be overcome in the digital world by simply making a copy of the original document before marking it up, ensuring that they always have an 'un-damaged' copy of the original file. A more efficient method of achieving the same effect, however, would be to save all document annotations separately to the main document. This would ensure that the original document remains unchanged, while at the same time facilitating toggleable annotations. It has been noted in previous investigations that annotations are often perceived as

"a separate layer of the document."   — O'Hara and Sellen [1997]

Therefore, separating annotations from the original text seems a logical step to take. Another advantage of separating the notes from the original document content is to allow multiple annotation files to be associated with a single document, allowing many versions of annotations to be viewed while only needing a single copy of the original text.

In our design, after a set of notes and/or annotations has been created, the program allows them to be saved to a file that is independent of the document itself—this will be known as an annotation file. A document can have several of these files associated with it, each of which can be given a different name and saved separately. The result of this is a standard format of annotation that can be created, viewed, and edited easily without altering the document itself. Consequently, these files form a template which can be shared among computers without the need to have multiple copies of the same source text.

Sometimes it is beneficial to purchase a professionally annotated version of a classic book to aid in the understanding of the text. Many companies produce scholarly editions of popular books, but to view them all the reader must in turn buy several copies of the original text. Similarly, if a reader makes notes on an electronic document and wants to share the document with others, they must not only send the annotations, but also the original document along with it. With the system proposed here, however, users can open any number of annotation files while owning only one copy of the original text.

To make the system complete, we also incorporated a suite of additional annotation tools into the design, which included: a note function, highlighter, free-hand pen, image box, text box, and repositionable PDF area. Users can also toggle easily between multiple annotation files (e.g., from other people) if desired.

To confirm that additional marginal space is indeed a lightweight property digitally, we conducted a comparative user study of our digital design. Participants in the study used our new interface to annotate and make notes about a number of digital books. They appreciated the ability to be able to use multiple annotation files, and widely used both the margins and the document area itself to make notes.

The full set of tools was used to annotate the document, in line with previous findings on the anatomy of physical annotations (see section 4.3.1). Where annotations were placed varied dramatically depending upon which tool was being tested, however. For example, 75% of participants felt that the text box tool was better suited to the margin as opposed to the document due to the difficulties of text occlusion on the document and the lack of free space available to place the object, whereas 100% of participants chose to use the pen and highlighter tools only on the document itself as opposed to the workspace areas. These results imply that using the margin of the document as an annotation area is not an *alternative* to marking the document, but rather a useful *addition* to it.

The highlighter tool was designed specifically to include the benefits of separate note-taking mediums, while at the same time overcoming some of the problems associated with their usage. That is, highlighter marks are semi-transparent so as not to obscure the original text, but they also allow text to be added and viewed as a pop-up when hovered over with a mouse. This not only eliminates the problem of orphan annotations, by ensuring that each one is referenced to its relative highlights, but also eliminates the possibility of annotations getting lost or detached from the original text.

The highly desirable feature of not obscuring the original text was a major factor in the mouse-over pop-ups' popularity, with 63% of participants selecting the highlighter as their favorite tool. In summary, then, the mouse-over note function is a popular and, more importantly, non-intrusive method of marking up digital documents, suggesting that it is a potentially advantageous replacement to the separate medium used so often in paper documents.

A more in-depth discussion of this study can be found in our accompanying paper [Pearson et al., 2009a].

4.3.3   LIGHTWEIGHT PROPERTIES

Observed behavior and participants' comments from our annotation study have demonstrated that

> • Document *margins* are a valuable and popular asset in the annotation process. The results of the study of our new lightweight annotations design strongly suggest that the margins are a useful addition to marking up the document as opposed to a straightforward alternative.

In addition to this, the study also strengthened the findings from our previous investigation into lightweight placeholding, confirming that

> • Mouse-over pop-ups are a lightweight way of displaying information that is not constantly needed. In this case, it is used as an alternative to the separate medium approach seen in physical annotation practices.

During the physical annotation evaluation we observed users making use of one tool for two functions. For example, some participants were seen using a sticky note as a bookmark, but also writing text on it, too. With this in mind, it may be possible to amalgamate two tools into one to reduce the total number of tools required—as is the case on paper. For example, the pen tool and highlighter tool need not be separate—as long as it is possible to change the thickness and opacity, they are essentially the same entity, and could therefore be merged into a single tool. Conversely, it may also be possible to create a sticky note that also doubles up as a placeholder, much like the physical example in Figure 4.1(d). Here, then, we suggest that

> • The concept of appropriation may be a lightweight feature that can be transferred to the digital plane.

In our example annotation system, user annotations are saved separately to the original document, which not only ensures that the document does not get 'damaged,' but also allows multiple annotation files to be associated with a single document. A small addition to the design included a toggleable dialog box that allows easy transition between the different annotation files associated with the open document. The subjective results from the participants on this portion of the study were promising, as the majority of the participants agreed that this feature offered several potential benefits to the overall active reading experience.

It is clear that saving annotations independently of the document both ensures that the original document remains unchanged and also allows more than one set of annotation files to be associated with a single copy of the original document. Therefore:

- Saving any user additions to a document separately to the document itself ensures the original does not get 'damaged,' while allowing multiple annotation files to be used and shared easily, and requiring physical storage of only one copy of the original document.

4.4 NOTE-TAKING

When undertaking active reading using physical books, it is common for users to make notes on spare paper, sticky notes, or other material. This additional media can also be used to mark positions within the book for relocation later; that is, to act as a placeholder. In this situation, the separate medium is dual functioning—it is acting as a placeholder as well as a note-taking facility. On paper this makes sense; for example, it would be unlikely for someone to make notes using a pile of sticky notes and a separate pile of bookmarks when one of these could easily do both jobs. Digitally, however, note-taking and placeholding functions are typically split into two distinct tools which, unfortunately, tend to suffer from a range of usability issues. Digital placeholders, for example, are a world away from what we are used to in physical books. As we have previously discussed, the way in which digital bookmarks are presented seriously affects the way in which they are used. In fact, the literature on this topic confirms their low usage within digital document readers as well as web browsers. Furthermore, the digital annotation tools we discussed in the previous section are also lacking in some areas. For example, the lack of marginal space on the majority of digital document annotation tools hinders the annotation process.

In this section we investigate lightweight note-taking, describing a new system that combines placeholding and annotation into a single unified tool, as well as incorporating additional static space for notes and a drag-and-drop interface for note creation and deletion.

4.4.1 BACKGROUND

When performing active reading on paper, it is likely that the central document will be used in conjunction with a multitude of other tools and equipment (e.g., pens, notebooks, bookmarks, etc.). This behavior has been observed by many researchers in the past:

"Paper is rarely used in isolation from other artifacts. Most often it is used as part of a collection of various paper documents, writing devices, and other information sources, even digital displays."   — Luff et al. [2007]

Clearly, the active reading process requires more than a mere document. The use of additional equipment and the availability of a suitable workspace to arrange material are common features in a paper-based reading environment, but these elements are altogether different when digitized. On paper, the ability to lay information out in a physical space is extremely important for the active reading process [Sellen and Harper, 2003], yet digitally, little consideration is given to the provision of an additional work area to make notes.

One of the major aims of our next lightweight active reading implementation was to provide users with a static workspace that enables them to integrate reading with other on-going activities [O'Hara, 1996] and facilitate the spatial organization that comes naturally when working on paper. By applying physical interactions such as this into the design of an improved digital active reading system, we hoped to provide familiar interactions which could in turn increase user satisfaction with the system.

Issues Associated with Digital Note-taking

Space: Figure 4.11, which shows an example of how note-taking is commonly performed on paper, demonstrates how the desk area surrounding the book is often used to keep notes that remain in place regardless of the currently open page. Although this concept of marginal space is seen in some digital systems (e.g., Adobe's Illustrator has space surrounding its canvas area to place objects), it is not generally incorporated into document annotation software. Since there is no comparable workspace in most digital note-taking interfaces, users are forced to make any necessary notes within the borders of the document itself. We believe this to be one potential contributory factor to the poor uptake of digital annotation tools, and one that, if suitably solved, could be considered a lightweight attribute.

Tool overload: On paper, it is common for one tool to have multiple functions. For example, a ruler can be used to measure as well as to draw straight lines. This property is often known as *appropriation* [Dix, 2007], and can be neatly described as improvisation, adaption, and adoption of technology in a way that its original designers may never have envisaged. Although the concept of appropriation is a common occurrence in the physical world (e.g., a heavy text book could be used to press flowers or to prop a door open in addition to its reading usage), it is rarely seen within the digital document domain. As Figure 4.11 illustrates, physical sticky (or 'Post-it') notes can be used in a manner of different ways:

1. Being stuck to a page within the document, which is useful for making notes about a specific paragraph;

2. Being stuck completely outside the document, in this case, on the desk, which is useful for providing static access to notes independent of the currently open page (e.g., as a book summary or similar);

3. Being stuck to the edge of a page, which causes it to act as a bookmark.

Thus, one tool is, in effect, performing two distinct functions—acting as a note-taking facility as well as a placeholding tool, something that in the digital world is typically achieved with two separate, and often poorly implemented functions.

Menu navigation: As we saw earlier, when a user is engaged in an active reading task, it is vital that they devote as much time as possible to the main task and not to the tools that are being used to facilitate it (ready-to-hand as opposed to present-at-hand). Hiding important tools within click menu structures, for example, may cause unnecessary attention to be paid to the tools themselves and not the primary active reading task. To help achieve a state of flow with the main task, then, it is important to achieve direct

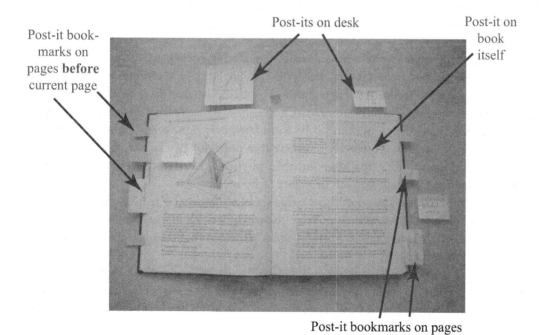

Post-its on desk

Post-it on book itself

Post-it bookmarks on pages **before** current page

Post-it bookmarks on pages **after** current page

Figure 4.11: An example of Post-its being used in a physical book.

manipulation [Shneiderman and Plaisant, 2004] wherever possible by reducing the on-screen menu system.

Scenario

The following scenario illustrates the common paper-based work practices of a young student who regularly undertakes homework at a desk.

Thomas, a 12 year old, is studying a range of subjects in school, and comes home every night with homework from multiple classes. In his bedroom he has his own desk, where he spreads out his books and assignments ready to complete his homework for the evening. Despite the untidiness of his work-space, Thomas has his own system for remembering and completing homework assignments that can spread over several semesters. For example, on the wall directly above his desk sits a cork pinboard that contains numerous items including to-do lists, permission forms, and time-tables. On the desk itself sit piles of books and paperwork, along with a variety of Post-its that are stuck to drawers, lamps, and pen pots. Looking closer at the textbooks on the desk, you can see scrap paper and Post-its sticking out—usually with hand-written notes and doodles drawn on them. Within textbooks you can also see Post-its stuck to individual pages with notes made on them—for example, in a history book there is a note on page 72 that says "learn 4 test fri".

Thomas's behavior is typical to many users of physical documents. By utilizing the static space surrounding his reading material (i.e., walls, desk, lamp, etc.), he creates an environment where he can view important information at a glance. For example, when he is reading a textbook and wants to quickly find out when the homework is due, he can simply look up to his timetable on the pinboard above him—an action that can be considered very lightweight. Alternatively, Thomas may have this information recorded somewhere in a notebook or planner, which would require the extra step of first finding the item and then physically navigating to the correct page—an action that could easily break him out of a state of flow.

When applied to digital documents, this problem persists. For example, when reading a digital document, the reader is likely to have to switch between programs or windows to locate information about their timetable, which is again an action that could easily break them out of their train of thought.

Thomas's methods for making notes and bookmarking pages within textbooks is also interesting. Specifically, to avoid marking or damaging what is clearly a borrowed school book, he makes notes on scrap paper and sticky Post-it notes and fixes them close to the area to which they relate. In many cases he also uses these notes as rudimentary page holders, making regular use of Post-its to stick to the sides of important pages.

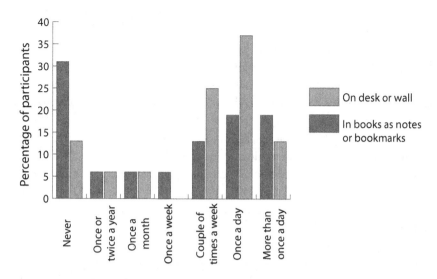

Figure 4.12: Users' Post-it and scrap paper use.

Current Note-taking Use

Previous work has not fully explored the frequency of paper-based Post-it or other paper note-taking use. In order to determine how these forms of notes are used, we performed a small user study, asking participants to report on their current usage of these paper-based tools.

Figure 4.12 shows the results of the study, indicating a diverse range of behaviors, with the majority of people using paper-based additional notes frequently (i.e., at least a couple of times a week). The results also indicate that the desk or wall is a common place to position notes—of all the people in our study making frequent use of notes, 81% placed them on their desk or wall, compared with 50% who used them in books as notes or bookmarks. Such a high proportion of users placing notes on the area surrounding the document suggests that space outside the document is perhaps more important than previously thought for digital active reading. This is also backed up by comments made by people we questioned: "I often use Post-its to make quick calculations. I leave them on the desk then refer to them later" and "I use my notebook quite often to write down page numbers and paragraphs of interesting stuff I'm reading. Obviously I'm not going to write this on the actual book. It's nice anyway to have a list of all the books I'm reading and all the pages that are useful on one sheet."

4.4.2 LIGHTWEIGHT NOTE-TAKING

To explore the possibility for lightweight note-taking around the document area, we created a system that incorporates both placeholding and annotation into a single unified tool. The *Digital Reading Desk* [Pearson et al., 2012b] also incorporates a large workspace comparable to a physical desk or wall for the addition of static notes, and a direct manipulation interaction style to reduce the time and effort required to create and delete Post-its. Although the system mirrors some of the properties of paper, it also avoids its natural limitations: for example, the Post-it piles are unlimited and can be resized and changed in color.

Drawing from the properties of paper-based reading (Figure 4.11), the document on the desk is a double page spread that opens in the same manner as paper books: two pages are seen when the book is open, and a single page (front or back cover) when it is closed (Figure 4.13). This design creates a space around the book—a known advantage when reading in print [Pearson et al., 2009a]. We anticipated that visualizing document spreads in this manner would encourage users to treat the space more like a physical book, and consequently make better and more frequent use of the tools provided.

The Virtual Desk

To overcome the problem of restricted space for notes, we incorporated a 'virtual desk' into the design of our new lightweight implementation. This space can be used to place static notes, and has been designed to mimic the additional space surrounding physical books, such as the walls and desks described in the scenario in section 4.4.1. The virtual desk, shown in Figure 4.13, is a useful area for placing any notes that relate to the document as a whole (e.g., summaries or character lists), or notes that would be useful to see at all times (e.g., to-do lists or timetables). It is useful to note that the desk area belongs to the document itself; therefore opening a new document will give the user a new desk.

The Unified Post-it Tool

Paper is multi-functional: it can be used for notes or for place-holding. To reproduce this, we amalgamate the roles into a single tool for flexibility and to reduce learning time. The Unified Post-it tool follows closely on from the bookmark 'tabs' we used in our previous design; that is, colored markers protrude from the side of the document like tabs in physical books. The way in which the unified Post-it tool accomplishes two distinct tasks, then, is dependent upon *where* they are positioned. Specifically, if they are placed on the document itself they are just notes, whereas if they are stuck to the sides of a document, they become bookmark notes. To encourage more flexibility with the tools in the system, we wanted to ensure that there are no constraints when it comes to where the Post-its can be positioned. Consequently, the Post-its can be placed either:

1. Completely on the document;

2. On the desk next to the document, or, if the book is closed, in the area behind the document;

3. Protruding from the document, which causes them to act as bookmarks.

This functionality essentially means that one tool now performs three separate functions: to make notes on specific pages of a document (use case 1), to make notes about the book as a whole

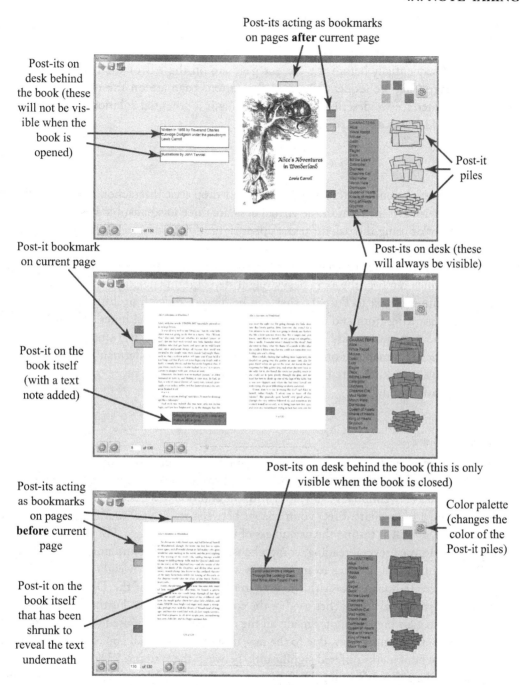

Figure 4.13: Screen shots from the Digital Reading Desk.

(use case 2) and to make notes that also act as placeholders (use case 3). Post-its that also act as placeholders not only navigate to the correct page when clicked, but also 'flip' from one side of the book to the other depending upon which page is open. That is, Post-its that are bookmarking pages that are sequentially before the current page are on the left of the book, whereas those that are on pages that are sequentially after the current page are on the right (much like the bookmarking interface we described previously). This is a potential solution to the problem of tool overload which was discussed in section 4.4.1.

Drag-and-drop

To reduce on-screen menu clutter we use a drag-and-drop style interaction for the creation and deletion of Post-its. On the right of the virtual desk are three inexhaustible Post-it piles that can be changed in color using the palette at the upper right of the interface. To create a Post-it, the user drags from one of the piles on to the document, on to the side of the document, or on to the virtual desk (Figure 4.13). Notes are removed in the same manner by dragging them back onto the pile, which removes the extra heavyweight step of right clicking and selecting delete. As well as the addition of text to Post-its, they can be moved, resized, or 'lifted up' (to reveal text underneath), borrowing from and extending the behavior of physical notes. All interactions are performed without menus: to add text is a double click, 'lifting up' is a single click, and so on. Removing the need for menus promotes direct manipulation [Shneiderman and Plaisant, 2004], and reduces the attention required for the tools themselves, leaving more cognitive resource for the primary active reading task.

Evaluation

To investigate the usability of our design, a short comparative user evaluation was carried out. Participants in the study used three systems—our new lightweight note-taking design, a conventional PDF viewer, and a conventional PDF viewer with the addition of a desk area. These systems were carefully designed to facilitate direct comparisons between traditional methods of bookmarking and annotation, as well as testing the usefulness of the static desk space. For each of the systems, participants performed several reading, comprehension, placeholder, and note-taking tasks.

Participants found it easier to make notes with our new lightweight system. It was also rated easier to create bookmarks with the drag and drop method of the Digital Reading Desk than the more traditional approaches used in the comparison systems. Furthermore, participants found it easier to view previous notes made on the new system, as opposed to the traditional tree structure seen in the comparisons, due to the new design's more visual appearance.

The use of bookmarks differed significantly between the systems: 75% of participants used bookmarks on the Digital Reading Desk system, while only 25% and 19% used them on the two comparison interfaces. This large increase in bookmark use strongly suggests that the unified Post-it tool actually encourages the creation of bookmarks.

The uptake of the desk area was also high, with many participants making use of it when available. For creating new notes for a *book as a whole* (i.e., summaries), the results strongly suggested that the virtual desk feature provided a useful area for positioning notes about a document. In the two systems where the desk was available, participants used it for this purpose 66% and 78% of the time.

A full discussion of this study can be found in our accompanying paper [Pearson et al., 2012b].

4.4.3 LIGHTWEIGHT PROPERTIES

The Digital Reading Desk implementation included an extended *static* workspace—a desk area that allowed users to make notes around the open document that stay constant independently of the currently open page. This investigation confirmed the popularity of the desk area, as well as showing positive differences in the patterns of use observed by participants in the open tasks, therefore:

> • The *static* workspace surrounding the document is a useful area to display constant information. For example, notes and summaries about the book as a whole or, in the case of our visual bookmarking interface, placeholder tabs.

Our second goal was to investigate the concept of appropriation [Dix, 2007] and whether designing for this usage can be considered a lightweight attribute. To achieve this, we opted to take two distinct digital functions (in this case, placeholding and annotation) and amalgamate them into a single tool to mimic the way they behave on paper. Results from post-study interviews, coupled with the patterns of use observed during our study, strongly suggest that the unified Post-it tool is an improvement over more traditional digital placeholding and note-taking techniques. Therefore:

> • Designing for appropriation, if conducted in a way that is familiar to the user (e.g., functions that are currently appropriated on paper) can be considered to be a lightweight property.

As well as these features, the Digital Reading Desk system also incorporates the idea of direct manipulation [Shneiderman and Plaisant, 2004] by creating a drag-and-drop style interface for the creation and deletion of unified Post-it notes. The idea behind this feature lies within the Post-it 'piles' that we designed to facilitate easy and familiar interaction from the users. In the physical world, users can just pick up a Post-it from a pile on their desk and place it on the book they are reading. Similarly, when the note becomes obsolete, the user can simply discard it by putting it back on the pile. To create a comparable interaction digitally, then, we have removed the need for any 'right click' actions by allowing Post-its to be dragged directly to and from their piles. The effectiveness of the drag-and-drop creation and deletion of Post-its within the Digital Reading Desk system was confirmed in the comparison study. Therefore:

> • Removing the need for menus wherever possible promotes direct manipulation, and is therefore less likely to distract from the primary active reading task, or interrupt any state of flow that may have already been achieved.

Finally, the visual overview that we discovered in our previous placeholders implementation was also detected, albeit to a slightly lesser extent, in the Digital Reading Desk interface. Although the new Post-it bookmarks have lost a certain amount of their ordering when compared with the tabs from the previous system (i.e., their vertical position no longer automatically indicates where they are in relation to other bookmarks), they do still provide an overview of where they are positioned with regard to the currently open page (i.e., tabs on the left are on pages sequentially *before* the current page, whereas tabs on the right are on pages sequentially *after* the current page). This overview was rated favorably by participants in the study. Therefore:

> • The visual Post-it bookmark tabs are a useful way of giving an overview of where each bookmark is placed in relation to the currently open page.

4.5   VISUAL INDEXING

A common activity when undertaking research, and indeed within everyday life, is the process of locating relevant information within documents. Whether it be searching a textbook for a particular topic, or simply looking up a product within a store catalog, searching for information is an often tiresome—but necessary—part of the information retrieval process. In physical books, the process of recovering relevant information is supported greatly by the ubiquitous back-of-book index system—a classic, well-known structure that neatly lists key terms for easy document navigation. When books

are digitized, this feature can be enhanced by means of hyperlinks, but often this is not the case. The limitations of this type of document navigation are clear: they are time consuming to physically navigate to, and are also author-created, therefore restricting them to static terms that exist when the book is created.

In the digital world, tools can be used to aid in the recovery of useful information. For example, the text search feature can be used to quickly navigate to instances of a particular keyword within a document. However, this function can be extremely time consuming if the resulting list is long, and there is often no visual overview of where each keyword occurs over an entire document.

In this section we investigate lightweight indexing, describing a new system that combines the visual overview of the classic index, with the speed and convenience of digital searching.

4.5.1   BACKGROUND

There are several steps one must take in order to find a particular piece of information. Shneiderman et al. [1998] define these steps in their four-phase framework for text searches:

1. **Formulation:** what happens before a search takes place.

2. **Action:** starting the search.

3. **Review of results:** the results from the initial search.

4. **Refinement:** what happens after the review of results, before the user goes back to formulation with the same information need.

In this model, then, the user must first decide on their information need; that is, what it is they want to find out, as well as where the best place is to search for it. This is known as the *formulation* phase and is considered by Shneiderman to be the most complex as it involves multiple levels of cognitive processing. Following completion of this phase, users will then move on to the *action* phase, which involves physically starting the search. In recent years, this stage is typically achieved by typing in a keyword or phrase into an Internet search engine and clicking 'Search.' Next, the *review of results* phase is where users search within each resultant document to assess relevance in relation to their original information need. Finally the *refinement* stage is conducted, often by means of relevance feedback, to offer support for successive additional queries.

This section is concerned with the *review of results* phase; specifically, the query in relation to individual retrieved documents (i.e., within-document searching) as opposed to the retrieved documents in relation to each other (i.e., multi-document searching).

4.5.2 CURRENT METHODS

Before we discuss the design and implementation of a new digital within-document information retrieval method, it is important to review the methods that are currently being used to locate relevant information in documents in both printed and digital media.

Printed Methods

To locate specific information in printed books it is traditional to consult the back-of-book index. The following scenario describes a common situation where the index is used to locate relevant information within a large document. The index used within this scenario is shown in Figure 4.14.

Hannah wants to buy a new backpack, and decides to choose one from a popular product catalog. To locate the product she requires, she first turns to the back-of-book index under 'B' to find the entry marked 'backpacks,' which contains an instruction to look under the more general 'bags' section. Luckily, in this case the 'Bags' entry appears immediately after 'Backpacks' and is therefore easy for her to find. Once she has located the sub-entry for 'backpacks' she then starts the process of looking at the index entry to find all the pages in the catalog that contain backpacks. Thinking strategically, Hannah

Athletics Supports..980
Audio
• Accessories..1385
• Audio Speakers..1463
• Home Cinema Systems.......................1408-11, 1357
• Storage..528-32, 1466
Audio and Video Tapes...............................1385, 1466

B

Baby and Nursery Equipment..............1489-1524, 881
Baby Gifts/Clothing...22, 1145
Baby Monitors...1505-09, 1516

Backpacks..*see bags*
Bags
• Backpacks....................................467, 1004-09, 1611
• Camera/Camcorder.........................1204/5, 1213-18
• Children's Luggage/Bags...............................1020/1
• Holdalls....................................1002-09, 934-36, 1146
• Ladies'......................................1014, 1006/7, 1146/7
• Luggage.....................................1013-21, 1003, 1009
• Rucksacks...891
• Sports Bags............................1004-09, 1146/7, 1611
Bakeware..712
Bangles and Bracelets.........42-53, 22, 31-33, 65, 93-95
Bar Stools..241
Barbecues..866
Baseball and Basketball..938/9

Figure 4.14: Snippet from a popular catalog index.

realizes that although the first entry is on page 467, the next entry is clustered (i.e., 1004–1009) and is therefore more likely to be the backpacks section, rather than a single occurrence within a different product segment. She starts her search by locating page 1004 and browses sequentially to page 1009. While she is performing this action, however, she keeps one finger on the index page, which acts as a temporary placeholder and allows her to easily flick back and forth between the index and catalog content.

It is clear from this scenario that there are both benefits and drawbacks to printed indexes. The advantages of the traditional index structure include:

- An alphabetized list of topics;

- A good overview of where areas of interest are located within a document;

- The clustering of pages (e.g., 3–10) shows relevant 'hot-spots' within the document.

Despite these advantages, however, the printed index also suffers from several potential problems:

- It takes time to physically look up referenced items;

- The possibility of un-indexed items, or items indexed under a term unfamiliar to the reader;

- If an entry contains multiple page references, the user must flip back and forth from the index until the correct information is found;

- Errors in indexing causing circular references that never lead to page numbers—for example, **canine:** *see dog*, **dog:** *see canine*;

- References from a single topic distributed over several meanings—for example, **canine:** *12, 35–42*, **dog:** *45, 56–59, 73*;

- Inappropriate inversions, for example—**Woofer, Sub:**;

- Indexing from section headings as a result of computer-created indexes—for example, 'Working with Threads in Java' being indexed under 'W' as opposed to 'T' for Threads or 'J' for Java.

In the early 2000s, professional indexers Macmillan Computer Publishing conducted a usability study to determine how well indexes meet the informational needs of their users [Ryan and Henselmeier, 2000]. There are many known issues with indexes that make creating them a difficult process. Despite putting a large amount of previous effort into index usability, Macmillan still identified problems during their observational study. Among other things, they were surprised at what users were looking for; that is, that many users were attempting to look up entries that publishers never would have thought of indexing. Macmillan concluded from this that different

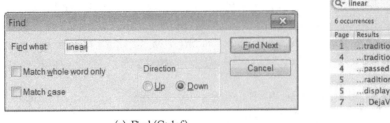

(a) Find (Ctrl+f)

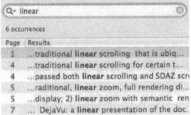

(b) Result list

Figure 4.15: Current methods of digital searching.

users take very different approaches to finding information in indexes—a major problem during creation, as anticipating the needs of everyone is obviously virtually impossible.

Clearly, despite their benefits, professional, statically created indexes still suffer from problems. However, some of these issues could be overcome by allowing users the ability to create their own custom indexes, a theme which is central to the new lightweight indexing method presented later in this section.

Digital Methods

When books are digitized, occasionally the index entries within are hyperlinked, allowing easy navigation to indexed pages. Unfortunately, however, even hyperlinked indexes suffer from the problem of flicking back and forth between index and book content. In fact, this problem is even more heavyweight on digital media as fingers cannot be used to hold pages, and the 'flicking' action is performed with the scroll bar.

The most well known method of locating information within digital documents is to use the text search or 'Find' (Ctrl+f) feature (see Figure 4.15(a)), which linearly scrolls through every instance of the search term until no more occurrences can be found. Despite being fast in execution, this method can be extremely time consuming if the result list is long, as every instance of the search term is systematically accessed one mouse click or keyboard shortcut at a time. This traditional text search method also gives no overview of where within a document each search term occurs, making it difficult for the user to pinpoint dense areas of interest. An alternative to the constant clicking of the find feature, is a partial result list like the one used by Apple's Preview (see Figure 4.15(b)). Instead of linearly scrolling through every occurrence of the search term, Preview returns a single list of matches along with a snippet of the text surrounding the word itself.

A limited amount of research has also been conducted into within-document search visualization. Jackson et al. [2002] for example, created a system known as SmartSkim which is based on relevance profiling—a technique that generates a profile showing where key terms exist across a whole document. The system uses histograms to give a within-document representation of relevant passages within a document based on a particular user query. Within each histogram, each bar corresponds to a fixed-length section (known as a 'tile') of text in the document.

Byrd [1999] builds on Shneiderman's [1997] WInquery system that displays relevance scores for multiple documents by creating a scroll-bar-based visualization for *within-document* information retrieval. The system covers the vertical scroll-bar with multi-colored 'dots' that correspond to keyword occurrences within the document. When the user enters a new keyword into the search, the program assigns it a colored dot, and places this above the other terms within the scroll-bar. A key of search terms and their assigned colors is then displayed at the bottom of the window. Although it can be difficult to distinguish between colors if there are many search terms, this approach does allow users to identify clusters of keyword occurrences by identifying areas of colored dots in close proximity.

The HotMaps system [Hoeber and Yang, 2006a,b] uses a visual representation to display query term occurrences using color on a 'heat' scale. Although this system has been designed to aid users in general information retrieval, it uses visual communication to help the user target the most relevant material more quickly. In particular, it uses color to indicate the number of times a word occurs within each document. More specifically, each search term is given a color depending upon the number of times it occurs within a document, that is, multiple occurrences of a query term (a 'hot' result) will be dark red in color whereas a small number of occurrences of a term (a 'cold' result) will be lighter in color.

As well as within-document visualization, there has been research into *how* to search within different types of digital document. Liesaputra et al. [2009b] conducted a study into searching for relevant information within different document mediums. They tested both back-of-book indexing and full text search on three different document types: realistic book formats [Liesaputra et al., 2009a], HTML, and PDF. The study investigated the influence of document format as well as search result presentation on the information search process. The results from the study showed that participants found information more efficiently and effectively with the subject index than full-text search, yet a post-study questionnaire revealed that the majority still preferred text search over the subject index. Despite the effectiveness of the index, then, users of digital documents are more inclined to use text search. This is yet more evidence to suggest that a hybrid system allowing custom indexes to be built from user-defined search terms would be a useful method of within-document searching.

Current Indexing Use
We performed a user study to determine current methods for locating information within both electronic and paper-based books. Figure 4.16 shows the results from our study of people who reported making use of physical (93% of participants) and digital (79% of participants) reference books at least once a week. It is clear from the results that the most common tool for locating information is text search (Ctrl+f), with all participants making use of this tool at least *once every three days* and 57% using it *more than once day*.

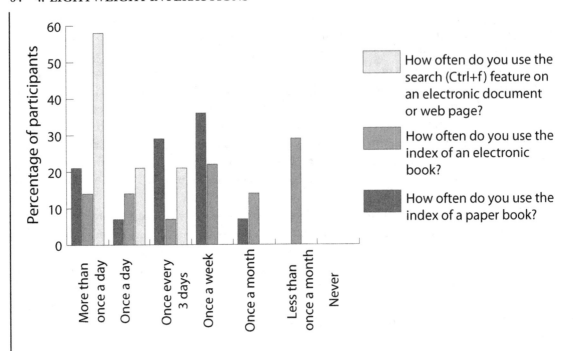

Figure 4.16: Usage statistics for digital search, digital indexes, and physical indexes.

When asked which system they found more useful within *digital* documents (text search or indexes), participants were quite evenly divided, with 50% opting for text search, 43% choosing digital indexes, and 7% selecting both. Although many participants commented on the usefulness of the overview that indexes provide, their usability was rated rather poorly. This evidence strengthens the argument that the traditional paper index, and indeed the imitated digital equivalents, are not the optimal methods of looking up information digitally.

4.5.3 LIGHTWEIGHT INDEXING

Taking account of the issues we have seen so far in this section, we designed and implemented a system that combines the visual overview of traditional back-of-book indexes with the speed of text search, while at the same time eliminating the need for flicking back and forth by including a dedicated index side panel [Pearson et al., 2009b]. The system, which allows users to build their own custom indexes via their own keyword or phrase, incorporates size and color to aid in the visualization of keyword occurrences (see Figure 4.17).

The foundation of our design is an index builder, which allows users to create custom indexes from their own keyword or phrase. It then displays the relevant page numbers (i.e., those that have at least one occurrence of the keyword or phrase) in chronological order. Its main features are:

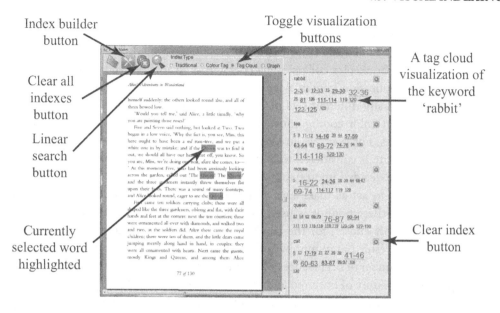

Figure 4.17: Lightweight visual indexing, showing the tag cloud visualization.

Page Clusters: To simplify the resultant indexes, the system is able to 'cluster' page matches. For example, when looking for all references to sofas in a catalog, the index may look something like this:

Sofa: 345, 467, **1067–1098**

That is, it will group major sections instead of listing each page separately. This not only simplifies the output, but also allows users to see the sections of the document where there are the most occurrences of the keyword or phrase they entered.

Hyper-links: Each of the search results in the system is the form of a hyperlink which when clicked will take the user to the appropriate page and highlight all occurrences of the keyword or phrase on that page.

Tool Tips: In additional to visual cues that illustrate to the user the most relevant pages with respect to others in the list, the program also has the facility to view the exact number of text matches on a page by hovering the mouse over a hyperlink.

To complement the index builder software, we applied several techniques previously found to be lightweight in order to enhance the visibility of the word occurrence data.

Color: Color plays an important role in the field of information visualization. There have been many examples of how color has been used to illustrate differences within and between documents. Bier et al. [2004] for example, use different shades of color to visualize which documents in a book-plex collection had been read. Ware [2004], in his book on this topic, describes an application known as *nominal information coding* or *labeling*, which describes how best to classify different sets of elements using color as distinct identifiers. He goes on to talk about color-coding conventions, describing the meanings of certain colors in different cultures. For example, in Western culture green is often associated with the word 'go' whereas white is considered to be the color of purity. In relation to the design for the new system, we decided upon two distinct colors that have conventional meanings within Ware's analysis to act as maximum and minimums for word occurrences. A gradient of colors between these bounds is used to illustrate occurrence values that fall within these values. The colors chosen for the labels, then, are based on a temperature gauge; that is, red for a 'hot' result (large number of occurrences of a query term) and blue for a 'cold' result (small number of occurrences of a term). Any results within this range will be colored purple (i.e., a mixture of both red and blue), the shade of which is determined by how close they are to the maximum or minimum values. This type of gradual color change based on 'hot' and 'cold' colors was also used in Alexander et al.'s Footprints Scrollbar [2009]. It is important to note that this gradient of colors varies depending upon the maximum number of occurrences of the keyword or phrase, but will be relative to that particular index term only. That is, a bright red link in one index term will be the maximum number of times that term occurs, but may well be significantly more or less than a bright red link in a different index term.

Size: Size can be a useful indicator to visualize the relative weights of different attributes; that is, an item with a high weighting will be larger than another item with a low weighting. In this case, it is desirable for users to see, at a glance, an overview of the most relevant pages within a document based on their keyword or phrase. With this in mind, we allocated pages with a small number of word occurrences (i.e., a potentially irrelevant page) a small size and those with a high number of word occurrences (a likely relevant page) a large size.

One of the main problems with the common index structure in digital documents is the amount of scrolling required to navigate between the index and document content. If the index is not hyperlinked, to look up more than one reference the user will either have to memorize all entries, or scroll to the first item, then back to the index, then to the second item, then back to the index, and so on. On physical documents this process is relatively lightweight in that fingers can be used as temporary placeholders so pages can be 'flicked' back and forth while looking up several index entries. Digitally, however, the process of scrolling is cumbersome and time consuming [O'Hara and Sellen, 1997].

To reduce the amount of scrolling required in the new design we opted to create a static index panel within the main interface that can always be seen while reading the document. This dedicated index panel is positioned to the right of the main document area, and contains a set of user-created indexes that can be easily deleted to maintain a clutter-free environment.

The page layout of the document in the system is *single page continuous display* (see Section 2.3.2). This presentation was chosen to allow quick and continuous scrolling across the entire document—a useful feature when scanning several pages for highlighted words.

Page Relevance

One of the main features of our technique is its ability to visualize page relevance. The relevance of any page within a document is highly dependent upon the number of occurrences of a particular keyword or phrase within a particular page, relative to the rest of the pages within a document. That is, any page with high occurrences of the user-defined keyword is considered to be more relevant than pages with low occurrences of the keyword, and is therefore visualized differently to indicate this relevance. Figure 4.18 illustrates the difference in size and color of the interface's hyperlinks according to relevance.

Visual Representations

Once the occurrence data has been calculated for a particular keyword, the program builds the physical indexes, which will be placed in the 'index visualization bar.' Items within this bar are rendered in one of three ways (see Figure 4.18) and can be easily toggled by using radio buttons on the program's toolbar. The purpose of these visual representations is to:

1. Display the pages or clusters that contain the user-defined keyword or phrase, in the same way as a traditional index;

2. Clearly illustrate the relevance of each page/cluster (i.e., how many occurrences of the keyword it contains) to give a clear representation of which pages are most relevant.

The basic structure of the index builder, and the base of all the visualizations, is a chronologically ordered list of hyperlinked page numbers and clusters. When the program builds an index, it first calculates the occurrence information, removes any pages that do not contain any instances of the keyword or phrase, then clusters adjacent pages. All links are then added to the index in numerical order, and all instances of the keywords are highlighted on the document. Each hyperlink is also equipped with a tool-tip feature that 'pops up' a bubble containing occurrence information when the mouse passes over it. Using the basic visual features discussed above, we implemented three visual representations of this basic index builder design: color tag, tag cloud, and graph.

Color tag: The color tag tool (Figure 4.18(a)) makes use of color as a visual feature. Although the size of each hyperlink remains the same, the color is changed according to its relative keyword occurrence value.

Tag cloud: The tag cloud tool makes use of both size and color to aid in the visualization of keyword occurrences. Tag clouds are traditionally chronologically ordered, size-weighted

(a) Color tag   (b) Tag cloud   (c) Graph

Figure 4.18: The visual index representations.

hyperlinks. In this system, each page or page cluster is ordered by page number as in the color tag tool, but is now sized according to relevance (i.e., the number of occurrences of the keyword relative to the other pages in the document). In addition to this, the color gradient used in the color tag tool is also utilized to further illustrate page relevance.

Graph: As with the tag cloud interface, the graph visualization also makes use of size and color to indicate page relevance values. In this case, however, each hyperlink is represented by a colored bar in a graph—the larger the bar, the more times the keyword or phrase occurs within its page or cluster.

Evaluation

We performed a user study of the three lightweight indexing visualizations (color tag; tag cloud; graph) in our new system against two alternative designs (standard linear search and traditional back-of-book index). The results showed that participants preferred the visual methods to the more traditional approaches, with the most preferred new method being the graph visualization.

The study also found that the visual systems were at least twice as fast as the traditional index, and nearly six times as fast as a standard linear search. There was no significant difference between the times taken for the three new lightweight methods.

The new designs were also significantly more accurate than the alternatives—participants found the most relevant section only 40% and 74% of the time using the linear search and traditional index methods, respectively, whereas the new lightweight methods were far more accurate. The color tag method achieved 95% accuracy, with the tag cloud and graph methods being 100% accurate. Buchanan and Loizides [2007] found previously that only in extreme circumstances will users be meticulous in their searching of a document while deciding on its relevance. We identified this behavior within the study—in the linear searching tasks, around a third of the participants did not cover the entire document before making a decision about the most relevant section. We believe it is this behavior that caused many participants to select an incorrect result when using the traditional systems.

Further details can be found in the accompanying paper [Pearson et al., 2009b].

4.5.4   LIGHTWEIGHT PROPERTIES

We created a tool for document indexing, a common activity that is currently heavyweight in both its digital and physical forms. For example, looking up entries in the index of a physical book is greatly supported by the use of fingers as temporary placeholders, but still takes time to look up, and also suffers from the potential problem of missing index entries. Indexes in digital documents are used in conjunction with buttons or scroll-bars, which can be difficult to manipulate quickly, and still suffer from the missing index problem. An alternative to indexes in digital documents is text search, which linearly progresses through each instance of a word in the document. This method can also be considered heavyweight, as it gives no overview of dense areas of interest and can be tedious and time consuming for words that occur many times. A key advantage of text search is that it does overcome the problem of un-indexed entries, as the keyword or phrase for the search is user-defined. When used in conjunction with techniques such as stemming and fuzzy matching, then, this method offers clear benefits.

The results from our user study showed that participants performed tasks significantly faster and more accurately using the new lightweight systems as opposed to traditional linear search. Participants also expressed subjective preference for the index builder systems over the more common text search. These results therefore confirm:

> • Giving an overview of where word occurrences exist within a document significantly increases both speed and accuracy of a search task.

This overview of important information is also benefited by clustering techniques that group consecutive pages together, as opposed to listing them separately. Participant comments on the topic of clustering within our study included: "It [page clustering] is nice—it's not very cluttered this way" and "I didn't even notice that—it just makes sense—like how books do it." This method of reducing the amount of information on screen aids users in the process of finding relevant clusters of information, which is a useful asset when attempting to locate specific topic areas within digital texts. We conclude that:

> • Displaying information in a more concise way, in this case, by clustering results, can aid the visualization of results to users.

Further, a comparison between index implementations found the new lightweight visual approaches to be even faster and more accurate than the traditional index approach. These visual approaches, which make use of color and size, were also rated favorably by participants in their feedback. Since the only difference between the visual systems and the traditional index system was color and size, we can therefore conclude:

> • Color is a useful way of visualizing important information. In this case, the color was used on a gradient heat scale to indicate to the user areas of the document with high occurrences of the search term;
>
> • Size is also a useful way of visualizing important information. In this case, the larger a link, the more word occurrences of the search term exist within the page(s).

One of the main problems associated with digital indexes is within non-hyperlinked documents, where there is a need to scroll back and forth between the index and its entries. Unlike physical documents, where fingers can be used as temporary placeholders to ease this process, digital indexes are usually used by simply scrolling to the first entry, then back to the index, then to the next entry, then back to the index, and so on. Although we did not investigate this issue during the study (as all of the index builder systems were hyperlinked), user comments such as: "It's great having the index on the side like that—now I can see the index and the page at the same time" and "It [the side index] is nice because I don't need to scroll so much" indicate that:

- Providing static access to important information, in this case the index bar to the side of the document area, reduces the number of steps users have to take in retrieving the information (in this case, scrolling).

Paper is not a panacea. There are many aspects of digital document design that, if properly implemented, can greatly exceed the limitations of printed texts. The intention in this case was to design a system that incorporates useful features from both the physical and electronic domains to create a digital solution that out-performs both paper and digital systems. This was achieved in our three indexing approaches by integrating the speed of digital search with the overview and accessibility of the physical index. Therefore:

- Mimicking paper is not always the optimum solution to the heavyweight properties associated with digital documents. We have increased both the speed and accuracy of locating relevant information within a digital document by incorporating the uniquely digital techniques of text search and hyperlinks into a physical index design.

CHAPTER 5

Improving Digital Reading

5.1 OVERVIEW

Reading is an age-old activity that is increasingly being performed interactively on screen. The soaring popularity of digital documents in recent years has been accelerated by an influx of electronic reading devices such as eReaders, tablets, and mobile phones—hardware that is becoming evermore fluidly integrated into our daily lives [BBC News, January 28, 2011; The New York Times, July 19, 2010; Wahba, September 22, 2010]. Despite the clear popularity of digital texts, however, research indicates that paper usage is in fact increasing [The Economist, October 9, 2008; The Trustees of Princeton University, 2009b], suggesting that people are obtaining digital documents, but are later printing them.

This underlying desire to print digital texts [Marshall, 1997; Sellen and Harper, 2003] demonstrates a clear failure of on-screen reading and reading related activities. It stands to reason, therefore, that if the motivation to print digital texts is due to the low quality of the tools used for digital active reading, then improving these tools would decrease the need for printing. How best to improve the way in which users interact with such systems, however, is a difficult task that, fundamentally, depends strongly upon the differences between paper documents and their electronic equivalents.

There are many key distinctions between electronic and paper documents. The tangible properties and affordances that paper offer are considerably different to those that can be performed electronically, resulting in a drastic variation in the interaction styles seen between the two media. For example, paper is thin and can therefore be folded and ripped, whereas current electronic screens, despite advances in technology [Lahey et al., 2011], are still too bulky to manipulate in this way.

The way in which physical documents age and mature, with help from their owners, is another key feature which makes them different from digital texts. Over time, physical books will wear, they will get tatty and dirty, often providing a nostalgic reminder to previous occasions where one's own copy of a favorite book was stained during childhood [Gass, November 1999]. As Marshall [2009] commented:

> "The tattered cover is, in and of itself, a reminder of the book and all of the experiences surrounding it."
> — Marshall [2009]

The act of annotation is a record of a reader's previous interaction with a book; along with general wear and tear, physical documents 'tell a story' that is personal to the owners that have come into contact with it. It has also been observed that in some cases, the annotations of others provide value to future readers Marshall [1997]. During a 1987 keynote presentation van Dam [1988] stated:

> "I would always grab the dirtiest copy of a book in the library, rather than the cleanest one,
> because the dirtiest ones had the most marginalia, which I found very helpful."
>
> — van Dam [1988]

The action of marking up documents in this way can be considered not as simply reading, but as part of a more focused and cognitively demanding process known as *active* reading [Adler, 1940]. Active reading typically demands more attention than what is required to simply read a novel or newspaper, and frequently includes tasks such as highlighting, note-taking, searching, and non-sequential navigation. It has been widely documented, however, that paper—thanks to its familiar and lightweight affordances—better supports active reading than on-screen implementations [Marshall and Bly, 2005; O'Hara and Sellen, 1997; Sellen and Harper, 1997; Tashman and Edwards, 2011a].

There have been many attempts to improve the usability of digital document tools by mimicking the interaction styles of paper. Chu et al. [2004] and Card et al. [2004], for example, have used the literal book metaphor [Landoni and Gibb, 2000] to create realistic visualizations of real books within their designs. Schilit et al. [1998a], Hinckley et al. [2009] and Tashman and Edwards [2011b], have gone one step further, by enhancing augmented reading hardware to create 'book-like' reading appliances. There have also been attempts to bridge the gap between the physical and digital domains by amalgamating paper documents with digital enhancements (e.g., Liao et al. [2008]; Wellner [1991]).

Evidently the physical properties of paper are integral [Luff et al., 2007; Sellen and Harper, 1997] to the ease in which they are manipulated, and undoubtedly contribute to the high proportion of users opting to print digital documents. A useful way of describing the physical affordances of paper is by what Marshall and Bly [2005] describe as lightweight interaction; that is:

> "... navigation that occurs either when people reach a particular page or when they move within
> an article in a way that is so unselfconscious that they aren't apt to remember it later."
>
> — Marshall and Bly [2005]

The almost subliminal interaction of acts such as folding, highlighting, and flicking require little cognitive attention from the user—a desirable state that is neatly defined by Csikszentmihalyi's [1990] theory of flow. The state of flow can be characterized as being so fully immersed in a task that all other considerations are forgotten. It is within this state of complete, focused motivation that users will achieve the maximum level of cognitive attention to the task they are performing.

To achieve the desired state of flow, then, it is essential that the tools designed to aid the active reading process are made as intuitive as possible to ensure that the user is thinking about the task at hand, as opposed to the tools used to facilitate it. That is, the tools themselves must be ready-to-hand [Heidegger, 1962; Winograd and Flores, 1985] rather than present-at-hand.

If the lightweight properties of paper hold (i.e., if the tools used to aid the active reading process are ready-to-hand), then a state of flow can be achieved with the primary active reading task.

On paper this ideal is often realized. For example, folding down the corner of a document to mark a page, or highlighting a word within a passage of text can be so unselfconscious that the user is unlikely to think about doing it. It has been widely recognized, however, that digital active reading tools are less intuitive and consequently require more conscious effort to perform, often breaking users out of their state of flow [Adler et al., 1998; Marshall and Bly, 2005; Sellen and Harper, 2003].

The main aim of this book has been to improve the digital active reading process by incorporating lightweight techniques into the design of new active reading tools. We have been able to show that doing so will make the tools themselves more intuitive, requiring less cognitive attention to perform tasks, and consequently helping promote a state of flow with the primary active reading task, a situation that is often accomplished when using paper-based tools.

Marshall and Bly's [2005] definition of the term lightweight describes the properties of paper documents as opposed to eDocuments. They speculated that this concept of lightweight interaction could be also be applied to digital technology but did not give any concrete evidence to support this possibility.

To gain a better understanding of what attributes can be considered digitally lightweight, we have demonstrated four example systems, each of which were carefully designed to investigate specific areas of potentially lightweight design. In some cases we closely mirrored the interaction styles of physical documents in an attempt to create a digitally lightweight equivalent, and in others we enhanced digital techniques to better utilize the availability of electronic functionality. In all cases, user evaluations demonstrated the lightweight properties of the new designs.

5.2 RUNNING THEMES

This section brings together the topics that have been prominent throughout this book. We use these long-running themes as a foundation to create a list of digitally lightweight properties for use within active reading systems.

5.2.1 ADDITIONAL SPACE

One of the main themes running throughout the example lightweight systems we have demonstrated is the use of additional space beyond the document. Superficially, this can take two forms: the marginal space surrounding document pages, and the static space surrounding the entire document (e.g., the desk or wall). These two approaches either give users extra page space for annotation/notes (the margin), or give support for the user's management of the document as a whole (static desk or wall space). This particular attribute has been seen in:

1. *Placeholders*, where *static* space was used to display constant bookmark tabs;

2. *Annotations*, where *marginal* space was used to make further notes and annotations on pages of a document;

3. *Note-taking*, where *static* space was utilized, this time, in the form of a 'desk' that allowed notes to be made independently of the currently open page;

4. *Visual indexing*, where *static* space was used to display an index bar to reduce the need for scrolling between index and document content.

The evidence we have gathered from studies of these systems and an analytical review of current reading technology has enabled us to confirm that the space beyond the document is a lightweight property that should be used in future digital reading designs.

5.2.2   VISUAL LANGUAGE

The way in which information is displayed is an important factor that can ultimately determine how effectively a system can be used. For example, if an important piece of information is hard to see or find, the user's attention will be shifted from their primary task to how best to access the information, breaking them out of their contextual flow.

There is a significant body of research that investigates the use of visual language such as color, space, and position to organize information (e.g., Marshall and Shipman III [1995]; Shipman III et al. [1995]). This idea of using visual language to display relevant information is also one of the recurring themes in this book. Specifically, these visual attributes have been identified in:

1. *Placeholders*, where *position* was used to indicate the location of bookmarks in relation to the current page as well as to other bookmarks, providing an *overview* of where bookmarks exist in the document. In addition, the use of *color* was also identified as a potentially useful attribute for distinguishing between bookmarks (e.g., red for important, etc.);

2. *Note-taking*, where *position* was used to give an overview of where sticky note bookmarks are located in relation to the currently open page, which also gave a certain *overview* of the bookmarks within the document. The sticky notes within this system also allowed their *size* and *color* to be changed, which aided in the indication of page importance;

3. *Visual indexing*, where *color* and *size* were used to illustrate word frequency within pages. The traditional index structure, which included clustered entries, gave an added *overview* of exactly where in the document important areas occurred.

We can conclude from the evidence gathered from these investigations that the visual language of reading systems is an extremely important feature for displaying information digitally. Specifically, the lightweight features of the visual language we have identified are: position, color, size, and overview.

5.2.3 IMMEDIACY OF ACCESS

As discussed previously, the desirable state of flow [Csikszentmihalyi, 1990] is achieved when an individual is so engrossed in a particular task that nothing else around them seems to matter. To achieve a state of flow with the primary active reading task, it is essential that all the tools that are designed to aid it are made ready-to-hand [Heidegger, 1962; Winograd and Flores, 1985], which ensures that the maximum amount of cognitive attention is available for the main task, as opposed to the tools designed to facilitate it. This will then reduce the possibility that the user will be distracted by the tools themselves [Pace, 2004].

With this in mind, it seems reasonable to consider the immediacy of access of the tools within a digital system. That is, how soon can the tools be accessed, and, more importantly, how cognitively demanding is it to use the tools designed to aid the active reading process?

One attribute that falls under this category and has been identified within two of our example systems is the idea of a reduced menu system. In theory, a system that has fewer menus will promote direct manipulation, and therefore allow functions to be performed faster and with less cognitive attention required from the user. The concept of a reduced menu system has been identified in:

1. *Placeholders*, where we identified that hiding contextual information such as bookmarks within menus is a poor design choice and can be considered 'heavyweight' if the function is frequently accessed;

2. *Note-taking*, where a drag-and-drop interface for the creation and deletion of sticky notes was implemented to promote direct manipulation of the tools.

Our investigations provided strong evidence to support the reduced menu system as a lightweight attribute of digital document design.

In addition to this, another useful function that has been identified as a lightweight way of displaying information that need not always be visible is the mouse-over pop-up, used in:

1. *Placeholders*, where hovering the mouse over a bookmark tab caused a pop-up to appear giving the user additional information about the details of the bookmark (e.g., the page number, user-defined descriptions, etc.);

2. *Annotations*, where mouse-over pop-ups were used as an alternative to the separate medium often seen in physical documents.

This function has proved useful for information that is not required to be visible at all times, but still needs to be regularly accessed. Allowing such data to be quickly revealed by simple mouse movements, as opposed to making button clicks or searching within menus, reduces the number of steps needed to access the information, and consequently the cognitive demand on the user. We can therefore confirm that mouse-over pop-ups are indeed a lightweight property of digital document design if used to visualize important but not constantly required information.

5.2.4   DIGITAL TECHNOLOGIES

There are many properties of digital documents that far exceed the limitations of the printed page. For example, digital documents can be searched, zoomed, and edited easily, providing a new layer of interactive possibilities that are difficult to produce on paper. By optimizing for these advantages, it is possible to create purely digitally lightweight interactions without the need for mimicking paper. Some of these properties have been identified in:

1. *Annotations*, where saved annotations were made separately to the main document. This ensured the original did not get 'damaged,' and also allowed multiple annotation files to be used and shared easily while only physically storing one copy of the original document. This idea of saving annotations separately to the main document is a concept that can only be achieved on paper through additional media loosely attached to the original content—a type of mark-up that proved unpopular amongst participants in our evaluation.

2. *Visual indexing*, where we confirmed that mimicking paper is not always the optimum solution to the heavyweight properties associated with digital documents. In this case, we increased both the speed and accuracy of locating relevant information within a digital document by incorporating the uniquely electronic techniques of text search, and hyperlinks into a physical index design.

We conclude from this evidence that the use of digital technologies can be considered lightweight properties if used effectively. In these cases we have shown that the use of independently saved file copies, text search, and hyperlinks are all lightweight properties of digital active reading systems.

5.2.5   DESIGNING FOR APPROPRIATION

Appropriation is a method of interacting with an object or technology in a way that was not originally intended by the designer [Dix, 2007]. Although it is near impossible to predict exactly how users may adapt a particular piece of technology, it is possible to design tools that support more than one function, mimicking the behaviors of paper. We have identified the concept of appropriation as a lightweight attribute in two of our investigations:

1. *Annotations*, where we observed users in the paper study making use of sticky notes as bookmarks;

2. *Note-taking*, where we created a digital version of sticky notes that could be used as placeholders or as a method of annotation.

Studies of these systems provided significant evidence that designing for *appropriation* is a lightweight property of digital active reading systems.

5.2.6   COMPLETENESS OF METAPHORS

A key point that has been evident throughout our investigations is the completeness of metaphors. The completeness of a metaphor is extremely important to the eventual success of any function that intends to support active reading—placing restrictions on what something means or where it can go is a demonstration of bad interaction design. The importance of the complete metaphor has been identified in:

1. *Note-taking*, where users were not restricted as to where they could position sticky notes. Notes could either be placed on the document itself, on the desk surrounding the document, or protruding from the document (which caused them to act as bookmarks);

2. Our review of the current state of the art, where it was evident that the lack of a complete metaphor hinders the interaction process. For example, page turning on digital documents need not be modeled on paper; if the designers choose to do so, however, then it should behave *exactly* like paper to avoid the incompleteness associated with a poorly implemented book metaphor.

We conclude that completeness is a lightweight property of digital active reading tools.

5.3   THE BOOK METAPHOR

There has been a significant amount of research that focuses on the visual book metaphor in an attempt to improve the usability of digital document tools. Although it is clear that mimicking every aspect of physical documents in digital designs is unfavorable and, in many cases, infeasible [Sellen and Harper, 2003], it is also apparent that visualizing documents using the physical book metaphor is a common design choice for consumers (e.g., in applications such as iBooks for the iPad) and researchers (e.g., Chu et al. [2003]; Schilit et al. [1998b]) alike.

The primary reason why imitating physical books within digital designs proves so popular is familiarity. This can include two elements: visual similarity and interactive similarity. Visual similarity, or skeuomorphism, need not in fact guarantee that the interaction is identical or even similar, and except as a (possibly misleading) cue that the interaction is book-like, is more an aesthetic than interactional concern. In terms of interaction, as most people have been brought up reading physical books, they will consequently find a digital text that looks and behaves in a way that matches their experience in print easier to use. However, it is very possible that a new generation of children being brought up reading *only* from electronic texts, on eReaders for example, will feel very differently about the book metaphor being applied to digital document designs. As Nielsen [1990] commented:

> "... it is unnecessary to keep the book metaphor except for walk-up-and-use situations where immediate transfer of past skills is needed."   — Nielsen [1990]

Features that are based on the book metaphor are not necessarily perfect in design, and can easily be overtaken in functionality by applying solely digital techniques. However, the familiarity associated with such a well-used medium is overwhelmingly strong. For example, in the absence of any better proposals, the first motor cars were designed to look like carriages, which were, at the time, a very familiar sight. Over time, however, these carriage-shaped vehicles were eventually overtaken, and cars now bear little resemblance to the once primitive-looking early automobiles. Yet there are few complaints from consumers that modern motor vehicles should look more like carriages. Could it be possible, then, that the integration of the book metaphor into digital document designs is merely a transition stage before arriving at a more intuitive, yet exclusively digital reading interaction?

One area where there is obvious space to move beyond the book metaphor is the use of different media. For a number of reasons we have maintained a focus on visual communication and annotation. There are also opportunities to include audio notes, tactile reminders and other forms of note-taking and feedback to digital texts. Indeed, using other modes of communication may well prove less distracting than overloading a single sense. This may well be a limitation of the printed book. However, there are downsides as well as advantages when other senses are used. For example, audio notes spoken aloud would distract other readers in a public space or library. Similarly, while tactile feedback is often attributed as a positive attribute of reading physical books, in fact current 'haptic' technologies capable of this level of granularity are relatively crude, expensive and rare. Therefore, only a limited benefit to a few users would be, at present, achieved by exploring that opportunity. However, any approach would benefit by considering flow and the interaction with the user's primary reading task.

This book has focused strongly on the transfer of metaphors from the physical to electronic worlds. By mimicking some of the interactional properties of paper, we have, in the majority of cases, increased user satisfaction with the tools available for active reading. Although this suggests that users are still not ready to completely abandon the look and feel of the physical book, we have also acquired evidence for the contrary by showing (in Section 4.5) how the physical book idiom can also be improved upon by using solely digital enhancements.

5.4 ELECTRONIC DOCUMENTS

One of the major concerns users seem to have with the eDocument paradigm is the fact that they do not actually own a physical copy of the book. Some of the studies we have conducted on electronic reading found that many users feel almost cheated by buying an electronic document, with comments like "I'd rather have the [physical] book because it looks good on my shelf." This electronic ownership of a document also causes other problems. For example, attempting to sell a copy of a textbook you no longer need, or even lending a book to a friend to read for a short while, can cause licensing problems for users.

Another issue with current digital reading technology is that the concept of 'pages' is not as concrete digitally as on paper. Although the familiarity of paper books causes 'page-like' breaks in digital media, possibly due to the fact they can be printed, in actuality, page breaks within digital documents can occur anywhere and alter frequently depending upon the zoom level of the document. This reformatting of documents, for magnification or otherwise, consequently causes not only the number of pages within the document to suddenly change, but also the page numbers of different sections of the document. If Chapter 3, say, of an eBook originally appears on page 40 of 100, changing the magnification to make the text twice as large will cause the document to increase in page length to around 200 pages. What was page 40 now no longer contains the start of Chapter 3 but perhaps the mid-section of Chapter 1; Chapter 3 may now start on page 80. This type of inconsistency then has a knock-on effect on other functions within these devices. For example, in some devices, bookmarks only record page numbers, not where specific page numbers start. Therefore, in the example above, bookmarking the start of Chapter 3 in the original magnification will bookmark page 40, and changing to the new magnification will not alter the bookmark to where Chapter 3 now starts on page 80, but instead continue to mark page 40—which is now in the middle of Chapter 1.

Clearly, then, using page numbers in this context is not a consistent method of referencing within digital documents. This is not, however, ammunition to completely abolish the use of pages from digital documents—far from it, in fact. The notion of pages are still vital for the use of eDocuments as they are needed for functions such as printing, as well as the potential need to reference physical pages to digital media. There is the need, however, to more concretely design for specific locations within digital documents to ensure consistency when the document is reformatted for magnification.

Other problems, such as the loss of paper-like tangibility within digital documents, have also been identified. Marshall and Bly [2005], for instance, comment on the failure of digital systems in the context of flipping multiple pages within a document, and the consequence of losing the serendipitous feature of simply opening a document at an interesting article. They also comment on the implicit metadata found within physical documents that often gives tactile feedback on information such as how much of the book is left to read.

Despite their current pitfalls, digital documents do have many useful qualities that, if and when correctly implemented, have the potential to overtake their physical 'equivalents.' Digital enhancements such as text search, zooming, and copying are all powerful features that significantly increase the usability of electronic text.

It is clear from several sources (e.g., Jackson [2002]) that some users feel that marks within physical documents provide a further contextual layer of information in addition to the original content. For example, borrowing an old book from the library and finding it has already been marked up with highlights and notes from a previous borrower provides another person's interpretation of the text, and may even help identify worthwhile sections without the need to read the entire book. In contrast, however, we have encountered evidence from some study participants that there are users who feel it is not at all appropriate to mark a physical book. In fact, some think it is a terrible, almost sinful action to take, even going as far as describing writing in books as a crime—suggesting that doing so may irreparably damage the books [Fadiman, 1998].

Digital documents, however, need not suffer from the usual problems associated with additional marking. In fact, not only can they avoid these problems, they can also benefit from other advantages, as well as potentially advancing in functionality by providing additional features. Although current digital annotation is deemed awkward [O'Hara and Sellen, 1997] compared to its physical rivals, our work in the area of lightweight interaction aims to bridge the gap between the physical and digital domains and hopefully make digital reading as easy to perform as it is on paper.

Other useful advantages of digital documents that we have identified throughout our investigations into lightweight design are the enhancements that can be made using the computational power of the reading hardware. Our investigation into visual indexing was designed to prove that it is not only functionality that has migrated from the physical world that can be considered digitally lightweight. The results of this investigation proved that the common text search function, coupled with hyperlinks and other useful techniques, can be exploited to produce a digitally lightweight function that would not have been possible on paper.

5.5 CONCLUDING REMARKS

This book has attempted to establish which properties of digital reader design can be considered digitally lightweight by creating and evaluating new implementations to aid in the active reading process. There are many ways in which current digital reading implementations are deficient and, as a result, many ways in which they can be improved. By incorporating lightweight techniques into the design of electronic reading software, the cognitive load required by users to perform document-related activities can be reduced, helping users achieve a state of flow with the primary active reading task. As O'Hara and Sellen commented, there is:

> "… the need to support quicker, more effortless navigation techniques."
>
> — O'Hara and Sellen [1997]

This statement encapsulates the goal of lightweight design within digital active reading systems. The main aim of interfaces designed to aid this process is to provide tacit and effortless interaction that causes minimal intrusion on the main reading task, or, as Marshall and Bly state, actions that are

> "… so unselfconscious that [the users] aren't apt to remember it later."
>
> — Marshall and Bly [2005]

As a general principle in human-computer interaction, it is important to improve the user's effectiveness in their tasks. As previous research, such as that by O'Hara and Sellen, and Marshall and Bly, has demonstrated, in active reading the main (and most important) task is engagement with the text. Increasing the amount of cognitive effort available for this task is therefore desirable. In this book we have sought to provide digital tools that require almost subliminal attention to control. Through this, more of the user's mental resources will be available for the primary active reading task. With this in mind, one of our main motivations was to prove by example that lightweight interaction is possible and effective in digital documents, and, as a result, produce a list of attributes that can be considered digitally lightweight to aid in future designs of active reading software.

To accomplish this goal we identified several active reading tools that can currently be considered 'heavyweight' in their digital forms. Specifically, these topics included: placeholding, annotation, note-taking, and indexing. By paying close attention to how these activities are performed on paper, we were able to identify what properties can be considered physically lightweight, and consequently apply them to digital interactions. From this core idea, we then designed, implemented, and evaluated several digital interactions that incorporate some of the lightweight properties of paper while at the same time adding electronic enhancements.

The results from these evaluations show that users prefer the new simplified systems over more commonplace equivalents. Not only did participants generally rate the new implementations higher than the baseline interfaces, but they also voluntarily offered corroborating judgements. For example, one participant in the study on note-taking commented: "I don't have to think too much about how to do it"—a perfect example of what Marshall and Bly describe as lightweight navigation, and proof that this concept is indeed possible digitally. Evidence from our studies also shows that the active reading process has been improved by the systems that include lightweight properties. This is a valuable contribution to the digital reading process—an activity that is becoming increasingly more commonplace [BBC News, January 28, 2011,M; The New York Times, July 19, 2010; Wahba, September 22, 2010].

Finally, from extensively analyzing both user behavior and subjective responses from participants in each of the user studies, we were able to compile a list of lightweight properties of digital active reading systems. These properties are:

Lightweight Properties:

- Space beyond the document
- Visual language
  - Position
  - Color
  - Size
  - Overview
- Immediacy of access
  - Reduced menus
  - Mouse-over pop-ups
- Digital technologies
  - Independently saved file copies
  - Text search
  - Hyper-links
- Appropriation
- Completeness of metaphor

This list of attributes is a valuable foundation for future active reading designs. It is our conjecture that properly incorporating these lightweight properties into new digital reading implementations will reduce the cognitive attention required by users to make use of the tools, and leave more time and effort available for the main active reading task.

Current digital active reading software is far from being a complete replacement for paper, but our research in this area has moved toward bridging the gaps between the physical and digital domains, making interacting with digital documents significantly less cumbersome. In this book we have shown how lightweight interaction principles can be used to improve digital reading—we hope that along the way we have also inspired you to use the same approach in your own future digital reading designs.

Bibliography

David Abrams, Ron Baecker, and Mark Chignell. Information Archiving with Bookmarks: Personal Web Space Construction and Organization. In *Proceedings of the 16th annual SIGCHI conference on Human Factors in Computing Systems*, CHI '98, pages 41–48. ACM, 1998. DOI: 10.1145/274644.274651. 49

Annette Adler, Anuj Gujar, Beverly L. Harrison, Kenton O'Hara, and Abigail Sellen. A Diary Study of Work-Related Reading: Design Implications for Digital Reading Devices. In *Proceedings of the 16th annual SIGCHI conference on Human Factors in Computing Systems*, CHI '98, pages 241–248. ACM, 1998. DOI: 10.1145/274644.274679. 2, 33, 34, 35, 36, 57, 95

Mortimer J. Adler. *How to Read a Book: The Art of Getting a Liberal Education.* Simon and Schuster, 1940. ISBN 0671212095. 2, 33, 94

Maristella Agosti, Nicola Ferro, Ingo Frommholz, and Ulrich Thiel. Annotations in Digital Libraries and Collaboratories - Facets, Models and Usage. In *Proceedings from the 8th European Conference on Research and Advanced Technology for Digital Libraries*, volume 3232 of *ECDL '04*, pages 244–255. Springer Berlin / Heidelberg, 2004. DOI: 10.1007/978-3-540-30230-8_23. 61

Maristella Agosti, Nicola Ferro, Emanuele Panizzi, and Rosa Trinchese. Annotation as a Support to User Interaction for Content Enhancement in Digital Libraries. In *Proceedings of the Working Conference on Advanced Visual Interfaces*, AVI '06, pages 151–154. ACM, 2006. DOI: 10.1145/1133265.1133296. 60

Jason Alexander, Andy Cockburn, Stephen Fitchett, Carl Gutwin, and Saul Greenberg. Revisiting Read Wear: Analysis, Design, and Evaluation of a Footprints Scrollbar. In *Proceedings of the SIGCHI Conference on Human Factors in Computing Systems*, CHI '09, pages 1665–1674. ACM, 2009. DOI: 10.1145/1518701.1518957. 86

BBC News. Amazon Kindle e-Book Downloads Outsell Paperbacks, January 28, 2011a. http://www.bbc.co.uk/news/business-12305015. 1, 93, 103

BBC News. Booker Prize Judges Sent e-Readers, January 28, 2011b. http://www.bbc.co.uk/news/entertainment-arts-12306173. 1

BBC News. UK General Title Digital Book Sales Soar to £16m in 2010, May 3, 2011. http://www.bbc.co.uk/news/technology-13262842. 4, 103

Eric Bier, Lance Good, Kris Popat, and Alan Newberger. A Document Corpus Browser for in-depth Reading. In *Proceedings of the 4th ACM/IEEE-CS joint conference on Digital libraries*, JCDL '04, pages 87–96. ACM, 2004. DOI: 10.1145/996350.996373. 86

Sven Birkerts. *The Gutenberg Elegies: The Fate of Reading in an Electronic Age*. Faber and Faber, 1994. ISBN 0-44991-009-1. 2

British Library. Turning The Pages, 1997. `http://www.bl.uk/collections/treasures/digitisation1.html`. 24, 38, 45

George Buchanan and Fernando Loizides. Investigating Document Triage on Paper and Electronic Media. In *Proceedings from the 11th European Conference on Research and Advanced Technology for Digital Libraries*, volume 4675 of *ECDL '07*, pages 416–427. Springer Berlin / Heidelberg, 2007. DOI: 10.1007/978-3-540-74851-9_35. 88

George Buchanan and Jennifer Pearson. Improving Placeholders in Digital Documents. In *Proceedings from the 12th European Conference on Research and Advanced Technology for Digital Libraries*, volume 5173 of *ECDL '08*, pages 1–12. Springer Berlin / Heidelberg, 2008. DOI: 10.1007/978-3-540-87599-4_1. 53, 54

BusinessWeek. The Office of the Future, June 30, 1975. `http://www.businessweek.com/technology/content/may2008/tc20080526_547942.htm`. 1

Donald Byrd. A Scrollbar-Based Visualization for Document Navigation. In *Proceedings of the 4th ACM International Conference on Digital libraries*, DL '99, pages 122–129. ACM, 1999. DOI: 10.1145/313238.313283. 83

Stuart K. Card, Lichan Hong, Jock D. Mackinlay, and Ed H. Chi. 3Book: A 3D Electronic Smart Book. In *Proceedings of the International Working Conference on Advanced Visual Interfaces*, AVI '04, pages 303–307. ACM, 2004. DOI: 10.1145/989863.989915. 26, 45, 51, 94

Jiajian Chen, Jun Xiao, Jian Fan, and Eamonn O'Brien-Strain. PageSpark: An e-Magazine Reader With Enhanced Reading Experiences on Handheld Devices. In *Proceedings of the 3rd ACM SIGCHI symposium on Engineering interactive computing systems*, EICS '11, pages 149–152. ACM, 2011. DOI: 10.1145/1996461.1996510. 28

Nicholas Chen, Francois Guimbretiere, and Abigail Sellen. Designing a Multi-Slate Reading Environment to Support Active Reading Activities. *ACM Transactions on Computer-Human Interaction*, 19(3):18:1–18:35, 2012. ISSN 1073-0516. DOI: 10.1145/2362364.2362366. 30

Yi-Chun Chu, Ian H. Witten, Richard Lobb, and David Bainbridge. How to Turn the Page. In *Proceedings of the 3rd ACM/IEEE-CS Joint Conference on Digital libraries*, JCDL '03, pages 186–188, Washington, DC, USA, 2003. IEEE Computer Society. 24, 38, 45, 99

Yi-Chun Chu, David Bainbridge, Matt Jones, and Ian H. Witten. Realistic Books: a Bizarre Homage to an Obsolete Medium? In *Proceedings of the 4th ACM/IEEE-CS Joint Conference on Digital libraries*, JCDL '04, pages 78–86. ACM, 2004. DOI: 10.1145/996350.996372. 24, 94

Andy Cockburn and Bruce McKenzie. What do Web Users do? An Empirical Analysis of Web Use. *International Journal of Human-Computer Studies*, 54(6):903–922, 2001. DOI: 10.1006/ijhc.2001.0459. 49

Samuel T. Coleridge. *A Book I Value: Selected Marginalia*. Princeton University Press, 2003. ISBN 978-0691113173. 62

Fabio Crestani and Massimo Melucci. A Case Study of Automatic Authoring: From a Text-book to a Hyper-Textbook. *Data and Knowledge Engineering*, 27(1):1–30, 1998. DOI: 10.1016/S0169-023X(97)00043-8. 22

Mihaly Csikszentmihalyi. *Flow: The Psychology of Optimal Experience*. Harper and Row, 1990. ISBN 0060920432. 40, 41, 94, 97

Mihaly Csikszentmihalyi. *Finding Flow: The Psychology of Engagement with Everyday Life*. Basic Books, 1997. ISBN 0465024114. 41

Andrew Dillon. Reading from Paper Versus Screens: a Critical Review of the Empirical Literature. *Ergonomics*, 35:1297–1326, 1992. 3, 35, 36, 44, 47, 48

Alan Dix. Designing for Appropriation. In *Proceedings of the 21st British HCI Group Annual Conference on People and Computers*, BCS-HCI '07, pages 27–30. British Computer Society, 2007. 5, 70, 77, 98

Michael W. Eysenck and Mark T. Keane. *Cognitive Psychology: a Student's Handbook*. Psychology Press, 2005. ISBN 1841693596. 41

Anne Fadiman. *Ex Libris: Confessions of a Common Reader*. Farrar, Straus and Giroux, 1998. ISBN 0374527229. 101

William H. Gass. In Defense of the Book: On the Enduring Pleasures of Paper, Type, Page, and Ink, November 1999. http://www.harpers.org/archive/1999/11/0060708. Harper's Magazine. 2, 3, 93

William W. Gaver. Technology Affordances. In *Proceedings of the 9th annual SIGCHI conference on Human Factors in Computing Systems*, CHI '91, pages 79–84. ACM, 1991. DOI: 10.1145/108844.108856. 43

James J. Gibson. *The Theory of Affordances*. Lawrence Erlbaum, 1977. 42

108 BIBLIOGRAPHY

James J. Gibson. *The Ecological Approach To Visual Perception*. Lawrence Erlbaum Associates, 1979. ISBN 0898599598. 42

Malcolm Gladwell. The Social Life of Paper, March 25, 2002. `http://www.newyorker.com/archive/2002/03/25/020325crbo_books`. The New Yorker. 3

Jeff Gomez. *Print is Dead: Books in our Digital Age*. Palgrave Macmillan, 2009. ISBN 9780230614468. 2

Saul Greenberg and Ian H. Witten. Supporting Command Reuse: Empirical Foundations and Principles. *International Journal of Man-Machine Studies*, 39:353–390, 1993. DOI: 10.1006/imms.1993.1065. 48

Wilfred J. Hansen and Christina Haas. Reading and Writing with Computers: a Framework for Explaining Differences in Performance. *Communications of the ACM*, 31(9):1080–1089, 1988. DOI: http://doi.acm.org/10.1145/48529.48532. 2, 3, 35

Martin Heidegger. *Being and Time (Translated From the German Sein und Zeit)*. Blackwell Publishers, 1962. ISBN 0631197702. 39, 94, 97

Steven Heim. *The Resonant Interface: HCI Foundations for Interaction Design*. Pearson/Addison Wesley, 2007. ISBN 9780321375964. 27, 44, 49

William C. Hill, James D. Hollan, Dave Wroblewski, and Tim McCandless. Edit Wear and Read Wear. In *Proceedings of the 10th annual SIGCHI conference on Human Factors in Computing Systems*, CHI '92, pages 3–9. ACM, 1992. 3

Ken Hinckley, Morgan Dixon, Raman Sarin, Francois Guimbretiere, and Ravin Balakrishnan. Codex: a Dual Screen Tablet Computer. In *Proceedings of the SIGCHI Conference on Human Factors in Computing Systems*, CHI '09, pages 1933–1942. ACM, 2009. DOI: 10.1145/1518701.1518996. 45, 94

Orland Hoeber and Dong Yang, Xue. The Visual Exploration of Web Search Results Using HotMap. In *Proceedings of the Conference on Information Visualization*, IV '06, pages 157–165. IEEE Computer Society, 2006a. DOI: 10.1109/IV.2006.108. 83

Orland Hoeber and Dong Yang, Xue. A Comparative User Study of Web Search Interfaces: HotMap, Concept Highlighter, and Google. In *Proceedings of the 2006 IEEE/WIC/ACM International Conference on Web Intelligence*, WI '06, pages 866–874. IEEE Computer Society, 2006b. DOI: 10.1109/WI.2006.6. 83

Lichan Hong, Ed H. Chi, and Stuart K. Card. Annotating 3D Electronic Books. In *Extended Abstracts on Human Factors in Computing Systems*, CHI EA '05, pages 1463–1466. ACM, 2005. DOI: 10.1145/1056808.1056942. 27

David J. Harper, Sara Coulthard, and Sun Yixing. A Language Modelling Approach to Relevance Profiling for Document Browsing. In *Proceedings of the 2nd ACM/IEEE-CS Joint Conference on Digital libraries*, JCDL '02, pages 76–83. ACM, 2002. DOI: 10.1145/544220.544234. 82

H. Jackson. *Marginalia: Readers Writing in Books*. Yale University Press, 2002. ISBN 9780300097207. 59, 62, 101

Richard M. Keller, Shawn R. Wolfe, James R. Chen, Joshua L. Rabinowitz, and Nathalie Mathe. A Bookmarking Service for Organizing and Sharing URLs. *Computer Networks and ISDN Systems*, 29(8-13):1103–1114, 1997. DOI: 10.1016/S0169-7552(97)00028-7. 50

Richard S. Krunk and Paul Muter. Reading of Continuous Text on Video Screens. *Human Factors*, 26:339–345, 1984. 35

Byron Lahey, Audrey Girouard, Winslow Burleson, and Roel Vertegaal. PaperPhone: Understanding the Use of Bend Gestures in Mobile Devices with Flexible Electronic Paper Displays. In *Proceedings of the 2011 annual SIGCHI conference on Human Factors in Computing Systems*, CHI '11, pages 1303–1312. ACM, 2011. DOI: 10.1145/1978942.1979136. 93

Monica Landoni and Forbes Gibb. The Role of Visual Rhetoric in the Design and Production of Electronic Books: The Visual Book. *The Electronic Library*, 18(3):190–201, 2000. DOI: 10.1108/02640470010337490. 3, 22, 94

Chunyuan Liao, François Guimbretière, Ken Hinckley, and Jim Hollan. PapierCraft: a Command System for Interactive Paper. *ACM Transactions on Computer-Human Interaction*, 14(4): 18:1–18:27, 2008. DOI: 10.1145/1314683.1314686. 45, 94

Veronica Liesaputra, Ian H. Witten, and David Bainbridge. Creating and Reading Realistic Electronic Books. *Computer*, 42(2):72–81, 2009a. DOI: 10.1109/MC.2009.46. 51, 83

Veronica Liesaputra, Ian H. Witten, and David Bainbridge. Searching in a Book. In *Proceedings from the 13th European Conference on Research and Advanced Technology for Digital Libraries*, volume 5714 of *ECDL '09*, pages 442–446. Springer Berlin / Heidelberg, 2009b. 83

Paul Luff, Guy Adams, Wolfgang Bock, Adam Drazin, David Frohlich, Christian Heath, Peter Herdman, Heather King, Nadja Linketscher, Rachel Murphy, Moira Norrie, Abigail Sellen, Beat Signer, Ella Tallyn, and Emil Zeller. The Disappearing Computer. *Augmented Paper: Developing Relationships Between Digital Content and Paper*, pages 275–297, 2007. DOI: 10.1007/978-3-540-72727-9_13. 3, 70, 94

Catherine C. Marshall and Sara Bly. Turning the Page on Navigation. In *Proceedings of the 5th ACM/IEEE-CS Joint Conference on Digital libraries*, JCDL '05, pages 225–234. ACM, 2005. DOI: 10.1145/1065385.1065438. 1, 2, 3, 38, 48, 50, 57, 94, 95, 101, 102

Catherine C. Marshall. Annotation: From Paper Books to the Digital Library. In *Proceedings of the 2nd ACM International Conference on Digital libraries*, DL '97, pages 131–140. ACM, 1997. DOI: 10.1145/263690.263806. 2, 42, 93, 94

Catherine C. Marshall. Toward an Ecology of Hypertext Annotation. In *Proceedings of the 9TH ACM conference on Hypertext and Hypermedia: Links, Objects, Time and Space–Structure in Hypermedia Systems*, HYPERTEXT '98, pages 40–49. ACM, 1998. DOI: 10.1145/276627.276632. 58

Catherine C. Marshall. *Reading and Writing the Electronic Book*. Synthesis Lectures on Information Concepts, Retrieval, and Services. Morgan & Claypool Publishers, 2009. DOI: 10.2200/S00215ED1V01Y200907ICR009. 36, 58, 61, 93

Catherine C. Marshall and Frank M. Shipman III. Spatial Hypertext: Designing for Change. *Communications of the ACM*, 38(8):88–97, 1995. DOI: 10.1145/208344.208350. 96

Catherine C. Marshall, Morgan N. Price, Gene Golovchinsky, and Bill N. Schilit. Introducing a Digital Library Reading Appliance into a Reading Group. In *Proceedings of the 4TH ACM Conference on Digital libraries*, DL '99, pages 77–84. ACM, 1999. DOI: 10.1145/313238.313262. 45, 62, 63

Daniel K. Mayes, Valerie K. Sims, and Jefferson M. Koonce. Comprehension and Workload Differences for VDT and Paper-Based Reading. *International Journal of Industrial Ergonomics*, 28:367–378, 2001. 36

Carol B. Mills and Linda J. Weldon. Reading Text from Computer Screens. *ACM Computing Surveys*, 19:329–357, 1987. DOI: 10.1145/45075.46162. 35

Paul Muter, Susane A. Latremouille, William C. Treurniet, and Paul Beam. Extended Reading of Continuous Text on Television Screens. *Human Factors*, 24:501–508, 1982. 2, 35, 37, 44

Jakob Nielsen. The Art of Navigating Through Hypertext. *Communications of the ACM*, 33:296–310, 1990. DOI: 10.1145/77481.77483. 22, 99

Jakob Nielsen. Electronic Books: A Bad Idea, July 26, 1998. http://www.useit.com/alertbox/980726.html. 22

Donald A. Norman. *The Design of Everyday Things*. Basic Books, 1988. ISBN 9780465067107. 6, 40, 42

Donald A. Norman. *The Invisible Computer*. MIT Press, 1998. ISBN 0-262-14065-9. 40, 43

Kenton O'Hara. Towards a Typology of Reading Goals. In *Affordances of Paper Project Technical Report*, Rank Xerox Research Centre, 1996. 2, 27, 28, 33, 34, 48, 70

Kenton O'Hara and Abigail Sellen. A Comparison of Reading Paper and on-line Documents. In *Proceedings of the 15th annual SIGCHI conference on Human Factors in Computing Systems*, CHI '97, pages 335–342. ACM, 1997. DOI: 10.1145/258549.258787. 1, 2, 3, 35, 36, 44, 48, 57, 60, 66, 86, 94, 102

Kenton O'Hara, Fiona Smith, William Newman, and Abigail Sellen. Student Readers' Use of Library Documents: Implications for Library Technologies. In *Proceedings of the 16th annual SIGCHI conference on Human Factors in Computing Systems*, CHI '98, pages 233–240. ACM Press/Addison-Wesley Publishing Co., 1998. DOI: 10.1145/274644.274678. 58, 63

Steven Pace. A Grounded Theory of the Flow Experiences of Web Users. *International Journal of Human Computer Studies*, 60:327–363, 2004. 41, 42, 97

Jennifer Pearson, George Buchanan, and Harold W. Thimbleby. Improving Annotations in Digital Documents. In *Proceedings from the 13th European Conference on Research and Advanced Technology for Digital Libraries*, volume 5714 of *ECDL '09*, pages 429–432. Springer Berlin / Heidelberg, 2009a. DOI: 10.1007/978-3-642-04346-8_51. 67, 74

Jennifer Pearson, George Buchanan, and Harold W. Thimbleby. Creating Visualisations for Digital Document Indexing. In *Proceedings from the 13th European Conference on Research and Advanced Technology for Digital Libraries*, volume 5714 of *ECDL '09*, pages 87–93. Springer Berlin / Heidelberg, 2009b. DOI: 10.1007/978-3-642-04346-8_10. 84, 89

Jennifer Pearson, George Buchanan, and Harold W. Thimbleby. HCI Design Principles for eReaders. In *Proceedings of the third workshop on Research advances in large digital book repositories and complementary media*, BooksOnline '10, pages 15–24, New York, NY, USA, 2010. ACM. DOI: 10.1145/1871854.1871860. 20

Jennifer Pearson, George Buchanan, and Harold W. Thimbleby. Investigating Collaborative Annotation on Slate PCs. In *Proceedings of the 14th international conference on Human-computer interaction with mobile devices and services*, MobileHCI '12, pages 413–416, New York, NY, USA, 2012a. ACM. DOI: 10.1145/2371574.2371637. 30

Jennifer Pearson, George Buchanan, Harold W. Thimbleby, and Matt Jones. The Digital Reading Desk: A Lightweight Approach to Digital Note-Taking. *Interacting with Computers*, 24(5): 327–338, 2012b. DOI: 10.1016/j.intcom.2012.03.001. 73, 77

Daniela K. Rosner, Lora Oehlberg, and Kimiko Ryokai. Studying Paper Use to Inform the Design of Personal and Portable Technology. In *Extended Abstracts of the 26th annual SIGCHI conference on Human Factors in Computing Systems*, CHI EA '08, pages 3405–3410. ACM, 2008. 48

Christine Nelsen Ryan and Sandra Henselmeier. Usability testing at Macmillan. *Key Words*, 8 (6):198–202, 2000. 81

Bill N. Schilit, Gene Golovchinsky, and Morgan N. Price. Beyond Paper: Supporting Active Reading with Free Form Digital Ink Annotations. In *Proceedings of the 16th annual SIGCHI conference on Human Factors in Computing Systems*, CHI '98, pages 249–256. ACM, 1998a. DOI: 10.1145/274644.274680. 3, 28, 94

Bill N. Schilit, Morgan N. Price, and Gene Golovchinsky. Digital Library Information Appliances. In *Proceedings of the 3rd ACM Conference on Digital Libraries*, DL '98, pages 217–226. ACM, 1998b. DOI: 10.1145/276675.276700. 3, 99

Abigail Sellen and Richard Harper. Paper as an analytic resource for the design of new technologies. In *Proceedings of the 15th annual SIGCHI conference on Human Factors in Computing Systems*, CHI '97, pages 319–326. ACM, 1997. DOI: 10.1145/258549.258780. 2, 3, 36, 43, 94

Abigail Sellen and Richard Harper. *The Myth of the Paperless Office*. MIT Press, Cambridge, MA, USA, 2003. ISBN 026269283X. 1, 2, 57, 70, 93, 95, 99

Helen Sharp, Yvonne Rogers, and Jenny Preece. *Interaction Design: Beyond Human-Computer Interaction*. John Wiley & Sons Ltd, 3 edition, 2011. ISBN 0470018666. 44

Frank M. Shipman III, Catherine C. Marshall, and Thomas P. Moran. Finding and Using Implicit Structure in Human-Organized Spatial Layouts of Information. In *Proceedings of the 13th annual SIGCHI conference on Human Factors in Computing Systems*, CHI '95, pages 346–353. ACM, 1995. DOI: 10.1145/223904.223949. 96

Ben Shneiderman and Catherine Plaisant. *Designing the User Interface: Strategies for Effective Human-Computer Interaction (4th Edition)*. Pearson Addison Wesley, 2004. ISBN 0321197860. 6, 22, 23, 72, 76, 78

Ben Shneiderman, Donald Byrd, and William B. Croft. Clarifying Search: A User-Interface Framework for Text Searches, 1997. http://www.dlib.org. D-Lib Magazine. 83

Ben Shneiderman, Donald Byrd, and William B. Croft. Sorting Out Searching: a User-Interface Framework for Text Searches. *Communications of the ACM*, 41(4):95–98, 1998. DOI: 10.1145/273035.273069. 79

Aurélien Tabard, Wendy Mackay, Nicolas Roussel, and Catherine Letondal. PageLinker: Integrating Contextual Bookmarks Within a Browser. In *Proceedings of the 25th annual SIGCHI conference on Human Factors in Computing Systems*, CHI '07, pages 337–346. ACM, 2007. DOI: 10.1145/1240624.1240680. 50

Craig S. Tashman and Keith W. Edwards. Active Reading and its Discontents: The Situations, Problems and Ideas of Readers. In *Proceedings of the 2011 annual SIGCHI conference on Human Factors in Computing Systems*, CHI '11, pages 2927–2936. ACM, 2011a. DOI: 10.1145/1978942.1979376. 94

Craig S. Tashman and Keith W. Edwards. LiquidText: A Flexible, Multitouch Environment to Support Active Reading. In *Proceedings of the 2011 SIGCHI Conference on Human Factors in Computing Systems*, CHI '11, pages 3285–3294. ACM, 2011b. DOI: 10.1145/1978942.1979430. 28, 43, 45, 94

Linda Tauscher and Saul Greenberg. How People Revisit Web Pages: Empirical Findings and Implications for the Design of History Systems. *International Journal on Human-Computer Studies*, 47(1):97–137, 1997. DOI: 10.1006/ijhc.1997.0125. 49

The Economist. Technological Comebacks: Not Dead, Just Resting, October 9, 2008. `http://www.economist.com/node/12381449`. 2, 93

The New York Times. E-books Top Hardcovers at Amazon, July 19 2010. `http://www.nytimes.com/2010/07/20/technology/20kindle.html`. 1, 4, 93, 103

The Trustees of Princeton University. The e-Reader Pilot at Princeton, 2009a. `http://www.princeton.edu/ereaderpilot/eReaderFinalReportLong.pdf`. 1

The Trustees of Princeton University. Why we are Doing an e-Reader Pilot, 2009b. `http://www.princeton.edu/ereaderpilot/rationale`. 2, 93

Andries van Dam. Hypertext '87 Keynote Address. *Communications of the ACM*, 31(7):887–895, 1988. 94

Phil Wahba. e-Readers Gain Traction, Spur Sales: Poll, September 22, 2010. `http://www.reuters.com/article/2010/09/22/us-books-ereaders-poll-idUSTRE68L3RG20100922`. Reuters. 1, 93, 103

Colin Ware. *Information Visualization: Perception for Design*. Morgan Kaufmann Publishers, 2004. ISBN 1558608192. 86

Erik Wästlund, Henrik Reinikka, Torsten Norlander, and Trevor Archer. Effects of VDT and Paper Presentation on Consumption and Production of Information: Psychological and Physiological Factors. *Computers in Human Behavior*, 21(2):377–394, 2005. DOI: 10.1016/j.chb.2004.02.007. 37

Erik Wästlund, Torsten Norlander, and Trevor Archer. The Effect of Page Layout on Mental Workload: A Dual-Task Experiment. *Computers in Human Behavior*, 24:1229–1245, May 2008. DOI: 10.1016/j.chb.2007.05.001. 2, 37, 44

Harald Weinreich, Hartmut Obendorf, Eelco Herder, and Matthias Mayer. Off the Beaten Tracks: Exploring Three Aspects of Web Navigation. In *Proceedings of the 15th International Conference on World Wide Web*, WWW '06, pages 133–142. ACM, 2006. DOI: 10.1145/1135777.1135802. 50

114 BIBLIOGRAPHY

Mark Weiser. Some Computer Science Issues in Ubiquitous Computing. *Communications of the ACM*, 36(7):75–84, 1993. DOI: 10.1145/159544.159617. 40

Pierre Wellner. The DigitalDesk Calculator: Tangible Manipulation on a Desk Top Display. In *Proceedings of the 4th annual ACM Symposium on User Interface Software and Technology*, UIST '91, pages 27–33. ACM, 1991. DOI: 10.1145/120782.120785. 45, 94

Ruth Wilson and Monica Landoni. Evaluating the Usability of Portable Electronic Books. In *Proceedings of the 2003 ACM symposium on Applied computing*, SAC '03, pages 564–568. ACM, 2003. DOI: 10.1145/952532.952644. 22, 47

Terry Winograd and Fernando Flores. *Understanding Computers and Cognition*. Ablex Publishing Corperation, 1985. ISBN 0-89391-050-3. 39, 94, 97

Hazel Woodward, Fytton Rowland, Cliff McKnight, Carolyn Pritchett, and Jack Meadows. Cafe Jus: an Electronic Journals User Survey. *Journal of Digital Information*, 1, 1998. 51

Authors' Biographies

JENNIFER PEARSON

Jennifer Pearson is a researcher in the Future Interaction Technology Laboratory (FIT Lab—fitlab.eu) at Swansea University, UK. She finished her Microsoft-funded Ph.D. in 2011 under the supervision of Harold Thimbleby, Matt Jones, George Buchanan, and Richard Harper.

GEORGE BUCHANAN

George Buchanan is a Reader at the Centre for Human-Computer Interaction Design at City University, London. His research interests focus on interactive search, mobile devices, and uncertainty in interaction.

HAROLD THIMBLEBY

Harold Thimbleby is Professor of Computer Science at Swansea University; he has been a Wolfson-Royal Society Research Merit Award Holder and a Leverhulme Senior Research Fellow. His website is harold.thimbleby.net. He is proud to have been Jen's Ph.D. supervisor.

Printed in the United States
by Baker & Taylor Publisher Services